Hit em Straight

CRACKING

the

CODE

THE WINNING RYDER CUP STRATEGY:
MAKE IT WORK FOR YOU

CRACKING

the

CODE

THE WINNING RYDER CUP STRATEGY:
MAKE IT WORK FOR YOU

PAUL AZINGER

2008 RYDER CUP CAPTAIN

DR. RON BRAUND

LOOKING GLASS BOOKS

Published by
Looking Glass Books, Inc.
Decatur, Georgia

Copyright © 2010 Paul Azinger and Ron Braund

Written in collaboration with Steve Eubanks and Dick Parker

Distributed by John F. Blair, Publisher

Photos by:
Montana Pritchard/The PGA of America: pages 6, 9, 14, 15, 29, 45, 51, 60, 78, 79, 118, 132, 145, 160, 163, 165, 166, 167, 170, 173, 174, 178, 180, 182, 183, 185, 191, 193, 194

Mike Ehrmann/The PGA of America: pages 17, 36, 58, 64, 76, 78, 79, 93, 130, 131, 149, 156, 157, 158, 161, 162, 167, 176, 177, 179, 184, 186, 189, 190, 192

Sam Greenwood/Getty Images: page 20, 116, 172
Andy Lyons/Getty Images: page 48
Harry How/Getty Images: pages 88, 153
Andrew Redington/Getty Images: pages 100, 138, 154, 191
David Cannon/Getty Images:page 107, 125, jacket flap (Azinger)
Ross Kinnaird/Getty Images: page 126
Tim Sloan/AFP/Getty Images: page 113
Morry Gash/AP Photo: cover
Lisa Weaver: jacket flap (Braund)

ISBN 978-1-929619-38-2

Manufactured in Canada

Book design by Burtch Hunter Design

To the 2008 U.S. Ryder Cup players,
assistant captains, wives, caddies, the PGA of America,
and our 13th Man, the American fans.

$\mathcal{A}$thletic events, big and small, often remind those of us outside the ropes that we all have the capacity to accomplish great things. The 2008 Ryder Cup fits that category. The United States team, underdogs in the eyes of many, played inspired golf for three days, sharing each other's triumphs and supporting each other during difficult times. As a spectator at Valhalla, I saw firsthand the strong bonds they built.

Now, in *Cracking the Code*, we learn of the behind-the-scenes strategy that captain Paul Azinger used to turn a group of individuals into a team. It wasn't easy. Among other things, Paul had to get these talented superstars to understand they would have to sacrifice their own goals for the betterment of the team. That mindset is crucial to success in almost any undertaking, including being President of the United States.

I have known Paul for years and have great respect for what he has done on the course and for what he has done for golf in general. Now I will add that I'm also grateful to him and the Ryder Cup team for the sacrifices they made to bring the Cup back to the United States. After reading *Cracking the Code*, which tells us how they did it, you will be, too.

GEORGE H. W. BUSH

Thanks to all who assisted in creating *Cracking the Code*, beginning with Steve Eubanks. A bestselling author who has written or co-written thirty books, Steve shared his talent generously with us in helping to craft the story. Also, the PGA of America and its photographers Montana Pritchard and Mike Ehrmann delivered much of the visual story of the 2008 Ryder Cup with their beautiful photography. Joe Steranka, CEO of the PGA of America, offered valuable advice and guidance at several critical points, along with Julius Mason, Mallory Crosland, Lauren Demary, Kathy Jorden, and Casey Morton.

To publisher Dick Parker, of Looking Glass Books, for direction in bringing the book to completion, and book designer Burtch Hunter. To Mark DeMoss and Michelle Farmer, of The DeMoss Group, for telling the world about *Cracking the Code*. And to our friends and family, particularly Patricia Zier, Joe Gaudino, Carol Gaudino, Mike Moran, Michael Hall, Rich Braund, Jeff Fray, Shawn Stoever, Charles Plott, and Bill Clark, for sharing many hours reading drafts and reviewing photos with us as we brought the book into being.

CONTENTS

THE CODE 3

1. THE FIRST TEST 7

2. THE POD STRATEGY 21

3. STARTING WITH GREAT 37

4. CREATING THE ENVIRONMENT 49

5. RELATIONSHIPS TRUMP ASSETS 59

6. GIVING OWNERSHIP 75

7. CONTROLLING CONTROLLABLES 89

8. MESSAGING 101

9. RELEASING CONTROL 127

10. FINISHING STRONG 139

CRACKING
the
CODE

THE WINNING RYDER CUP STRATEGY:
MAKE IT WORK FOR YOU

THE CODE

$\mathcal{G}$olf on the PGA Tour is the ultimate individual sport. If you don't perform, you don't get paid. You have no salary, and no team-mates to pick you up.

As Americans we honor the kind of individual greatness that golf spotlights. Every other year, however, we attempt to lay indi-vidualism aside and come together as a team, when the twelve best American golfers compete with Europe's twelve best for the Ryder Cup. Many professional golfers who have played in Ryder Cup competition will tell you the pressure to win for our country is greater than at any other tournament, even the majors.

For twenty-five years, beginning after the 1983 matches, the Europeans dominated the Ryder Cup, winning eight of the eleven events, even though we had been heavily favored to win most of them. The disheartening results embarrassed our players, yet no one seemed to have an answer for the Europeans. "Let's have no more talk about the Americans having the best players, the most major championships, the strongest team," the Associated Press wrote. "They are now the underdogs in this every-other-year matchup, unable to compete with the camaraderie, creativity, or fearlessness of their European counterparts."

A stinging indictment.

The PGA of America invited me to serve as captain of the 2008 United States Ryder Cup team. It was a daunting challenge. The last time we had brought the Cup home had been 1999; so much history on the course and off in those nine years. The 2001 match, scheduled for September 28–30, had been postponed for a year because of the September 11 attacks. We had not won the Ryder Cup since then, losing in 2002, 2004, and 2006.

To bring the Ryder Cup back to the United States, I knew, would require radical thinking: a team approach to a game dominated by individual greatness. Working with my friend Ron Braund, a life coach and corporate team-building expert, we focused on several key principles—the code—that work in elite military operations and successful business organizations:

➤ Break the twelve-man team into small pods of four players each.

➤ Place players in pods based on their personality types rather than on particular strengths in their golf games.

➤ Change the traditional Ryder Cup points system to allow "hotter"

4

players to win a place on the team. Also, give the captain four "captain's picks" instead of two.

➤ Control the controllables.

➤ Trust and empower assistant coaches and the players.

➤ Communicate with each golfer appropriately, based on his personality type.

Our players, along with their wives and caddies, embraced the code and the opportunity to become more than a team, and by the end of the week, when the United States had won the Ryder Cup by a surprising 16½ to 11½ margin, we were more than a team. We were a family.

We hope you will enjoy our story and then make our team-building strategy work within your organization to foster camaraderie, creativity, and fearlessness.

1

THE FIRST TEST

U-S-A! U-S-A! U-S-A!"

The cheers pounded my chest as the flags waved and Phil Mickelson's drive flew twenty-five yards past Padraig Harrington's ball, landing in the middle of the first fairway. It was barely eight o'clock on Friday morning, and already nine years of pent-up Ryder Cup frustration echoed across the Kentucky countryside. The game was on. More than a game, really. More than golf. The Ryder Cup is about country. About pride. The best of the United States versus the best of Europe. And in five of the previous six matches since 1993, including the last three straight, the Europeans had won the Cup. Year after year our guys had to answer the same questions about folding under pressure, playing uptight, losing despite holding a clear advantage in talent. Some

The beginning of the Ryder Cup competition offered both anticipation and hope. The performance on the course would determine the outcome in the quest to reclaim the Ryder Cup for the United States. The first American shot was placed in the hands of six-time Ryder Cup veteran Phil Mickelson. ~ Ron Braund

even dared ask if the American players cared anymore.

We cared. You look at the faces, you see the tears, and you know. We cared. We wanted the Cup as badly as any athlete wants any championship, for ourselves and for our country. And when this crowd, which had revved us up the night before at a raucous pep rally in downtown Louisville, thundered its approval of Phil's first tee shot, we wanted to bring the Cup home for them.

I stood several paces behind the tee as my counterpart, Nick Faldo, spoke to his players, and I remembered my first Ryder Cup. It was 1989 at The Belfry, in Sutton Coldfield, England. Nick and I already had something of a rivalry, at least in my mind. During Saturday afternoon fourball competition my partner, Chip Beck, and I faced Nick and Ian Woosnam. "I don't know about you, Chipper," I said as we walked toward the first tee, "but for me this is personal." I just wanted to beat the guy; I didn't want them celebrating at our expense. It took everything we had, 11-under par, to win 2 and 1.

Now here we were again, two decades later, Nick and I at the first tee, and neither of us would swing a club. I was captain of the United States Ryder Cup team; Nick was captain of the European team. I wanted to beat him and his team as badly as I had in 1989, but I would have to rely on my twelve guys and the plan we had laid out. The feeling was an odd one. When I held a golf club, I was in control. Win or lose, my destiny was in my hands. This time all I could do was watch. For two years, since my selection as captain, I had been working toward this moment. In fact, long before I was named U.S. captain I was considering a team-building plan that I thought would give the United States the best opportunity for success. I asked the PGA of America to overhaul

Nobody on the 2008 Ryder Cup team was more confident than the youngest player, Anthony Kim, shown here with his caddie, Eric Larson. Throughout the week Paul would tap into that confidence, and the fresh enthusiasm of all six U.S. Ryder Cup rookies. ~ R.B.

the way the Ryder Cup team was selected and managed, and the role the captain and assistant captains would play, and they had gone out on a limb and agreed. Now it was up to the players.

The Friday morning matches were foursomes, or alternate shot, with two players on each team. One tees off, the other hits next, and so on. Robert Karlsson, Harrington's partner, hit the second shot from the fairway for the Europeans, an eight-iron that he stiffed to six feet to the left of the hole. Then Anthony Kim ("AK"), one of six Ryder Cup rookies on our team, left his approach twenty feet short. Phil missed the long putt, then Padraig made his, and our guys were down one hole. In fact, by the time all four groups had played through one, we had lost the hole three times.

Two and a half hours later Phil stood beside the fourteenth tee box and watched AK drill a five iron straight toward the flag 215 yards away. The gallery, so eager for an American win, exploded with red, white, and blue whoops of joy and shouts of, "You da man, AK!" Not Phil. He knew. So did AK. Pumped up from winning the thirteenth hole after the Europeans had won ten, eleven, and twelve, AK made a great swing, but with too much juice. The ball would never hold, and the downslope behind the green made for one of the toughest up-and-downs on the course.

Cheers turned to groans and the dozens of American flags in the gallery fell limp as the ball rolled off the back of the green and down the embankment toward the television tower. The momentum was lost. It wasn't even noon on the first day of competition, and already the gallery sensed another American disaster looming. The first American pairing on the course, with our best player, was about to be three holes down with four to play against Harrington and Karlsson. AK glanced over at Phil as if to say, "Sorry, partner." Phil gave him a hint of a smile and shrugged a silent, "It's okay." AK had given Phil an almost impossible lie—even for the best short-game player in the world—in the most pressure-packed setting in golf.

I sat down heavily in the captain's cart. I had to say something. I couldn't just sit and watch. My guys needed a word of encouragement, especially AK. Not so much Phil; what do you say to a player with well over thirty tournament wins? He'd dug out of deeper holes than this one a dozen times, and he didn't need any advice from me. But AK, the cocky twenty-three-year-old kid with the infectious smile and barely two years on the PGA Tour, was another story. His

It was a privilege to join Paul as his advisor and consultant for the Ryder Cup. Here we observe the action on the course as events unfolded on Friday morning. One of my roles was to evaluate situations and provide information to help him message the players during the matches. ~ R.B.

passion reminded me of my own. AK took this thing personally.

"What do I say?" I thought out loud.

"Challenge him," Ron said. Ron Braund, sitting beside me in the cart, was a corporate team-building consultant who had worked with me to shape this team, showing me the principles of personality profiling and how matching personalities between partners could make an even greater impact on our team than matching golf skills.

"What?" I asked Ron, wondering how he knew what I was thinking.

"AK," Ron said. "You've got to challenge him. Get his attention. You challenge him and he'll respond."

Two years earlier I would have told you Ron's advice was a bunch of psychobabble nonsense. But as captain I had only a few variables I could control. The message was one of those. And the way I delivered that message had to change, depending on who I was addressing.

Challenge him.

I looked for the quickest way around the gallery to get to the fourteenth green, then I popped the brake and backtracked across the thirteenth fairway—there was no governor on the captains' carts, so we were flying—then through the rough beside fourteen toward the fifteenth tee. Slowing down to weave through the tremendous crowds was like swimming in syrup, but I finally found a break in the mass of humanity on the hillside behind the fifteenth tee. I jumped out of the cart, walked around the television tower, and caught them as Phil was examining the lie. It was even worse than I thought. Not only was it below the two-tiered green, it had ended up in grass already trampled by the gallery. You couldn't have walked it out there and placed it in a worse spot.

For a moment I simply stood among the gallery and thought about where we were. Over the last two years, at my request, the PGA of America had changed the way players qualified for the team, changed the Ryder Cup team selection process, and changed the order of play so that the matches began with foursomes, which historically had been stronger for the U.S. than the fourball (or "best ball") format. I had asked some of the most qualified and competent men in the game to be my assistant captains and then involved them in every aspect of team leadership. We had taken a never-before-tried approach to team building, and I had preached the gospel of preparation to every member of the team, giving them confidence in the fact that I had complete confidence in them. After all that and much more, the first group on Friday morning, Phil Mickelson and Anthony Kim, were two down and in deep trouble with time running out. I had to challenge AK, and I had to do it now.

I stepped over the rope, and AK, who hadn't seen me since he teed off, didn't say anything initially. I stood about four feet away from him with my arms folded. I looked at him and then looked away. When I looked back, AK said, "What's wrong, Cap'n?"

The place was almost completely silent as the gallery watched Phil size up the mess he was in. I didn't want the crowd to hear what I had to say, or to distract Phil from his nearly impossible task, so in the firmest whisper I could manage, I responded, "Buddy, I thought you were going to show me something today. You're not showing me squat!"

The trademark grin came back, and he said, "Relax, Cap'n. They're not gonna beat us."

Then Phil, who hadn't heard any of our conversation, hit one of the greatest flop shots of his life. From a place where most of the guys out there that weekend couldn't have gotten the ball within ten feet of the hole, he dropped it on the perfect spot to catch the ride down and stop three feet from the cup. In the meantime, the Europeans had their own struggles, bogeying the hole. AK made the par putt, and suddenly instead of being three down, he and Phil were just one hole behind with all the momentum.

One hole later AK hit a wedge to within twelve feet on exactly the right line to give Phil a straight uphill putt. When that putt fell, they had squared the match.

AK saw me again on eighteen, smiled even bigger than before, and said, "I told you, Cap'n."

These two photographs sum up in large degree the important balance of team building and execution for the success of the U.S. team. Phil Mickelson's amazing flop shot at fourteen on Friday morning was a reminder that even after all the team building, players still have to make the shots. In the opposite photo you see the team dynamic at work.

Now it was my turn to smile. "Yes, you did." He and Phil halved the match to earn the first half-point of the week, and the turnaround felt like a win. They had come through like the champions they are.

•

At the highest level of competitive golf, the difference between winning and losing is razor thin. One putt out of a hundred that lips out instead of going in is all it takes. That's true in most professional sports. Jeff Gordon says the difference between winning a NASCAR championship and finishing in the middle of the pack is so slight that most people never realize it exists. Major League

Anthony Kim spots the ball after the shot, and Raymond Floyd, one of Paul's assistant captains, comes onto the green to congratulate Phil. Raymond, a former Ryder Cup captain himself and a winner of four major championships, could not assist the players on the course, but he remained a constant, encouraging presence. All three assistant captains, Raymond, Dave Stockton, and Olin Browne, took active leadership roles throughout the week. ~ R.B.

batting coaches will tell you a one-inch change in a batter's stance can mean the difference between hitting .220 and .330.

Nerves are part of that mix. Nerves happen. You can't see them, but they're always there. You hear them in the quiver of a singer's voice, and sense them in the eyes of a student who gets a tough question. Nerves are all around you: in bouncing feet before the opening tip of a play-off game or the fidgets prior to the first pitch of a World Series. They're the churn in your stomach before a big meeting, the thump in your chest when you head down your first black-diamond ski slope, the knot in your throat as you ask for the sale. Nerves are as natural as rain on a rooftop. They are God's way of telling you to stand up straight and pay attention, something big is headed your way.

There isn't a golfer on the planet who doesn't know the feeling. You're standing on the tee needing a par to shoot a career round or beat a friend for the first time, or you have a putt to win a bet, or a match, or a tournament. *Focus*, you tell yourself. Then you take a deep breath and go through your pre-shot routine—visualize, practice swing, waggle—each step intended to help you relax. Whether you're an eighteen-handicapper who never plays anything more important than your local member-guest, or a PGA Tour veteran, you know the feeling. Nerves happen. It's part of the game.

I had gone toe to toe with nerves at various times in my career. Having a putt to win a major championship in sudden-death is a nerve-wracking experience, and I had survived that. But I had ten years experience on the tour by then. Now, like every U.S. captain since Jack Nicklaus in 1987, I was a rookie, and I had six rookie players on my team. As the golf cart I was driving plowed through the dew-covered rough on that clear September morning in 2008, I trusted our system and the relationships we had created to help us avoid rookie mistakes.

The Ryder Cup is one of the biggest pressure cookers in sports, and one of the few golf events that can bring the game's greatest players to tears. I had been there too, wearing the colors of team USA, standing on the tee with the flag of my country on my bag when my name was announced, and breath suddenly became tough to find. In 2002, the last time I was a member of a Ryder Cup team, I was the first player out in the first match on Friday morning. It was back at

The pressure cooker works both ways, and a leader seeks every opportunity to turn up the pressure on his opponent. On the tee at fourteen the American crowd makes its presence felt with Padraig Harrington of Ireland. ~ R.B.

The Belfry, and Captain Curtis Strange had paired me with Tiger Woods. As if playing with Tiger on the world's biggest stage wasn't enough, at least ten thousand people crowded into the stands and lined the first fairway when I stepped onto the tee. They weren't your typical golf crowd either. Thousands were cheering and singing, "Olé, Olé, Olé" at seven in the morning! When the starter said, "Now on the tee, representing the United States of America . . ." the hair on my arms stood on end. A third of the people, the Americans, whooped like it was a football game. The other two-thirds sat in stone silence. It was a surreal moment, one I'll probably never experience again, and certainly one I'll never forget. But once the gun sounded and we were off the first tee, my instincts kicked in and I was able to settle into my normal routine. Having played on four Ryder Cup teams—two wins, one loss, and one tie that left the Cup in Europe's hands—I had experienced the full range of Ryder Cup emotions. I knew the agony that coursed through the losers, and I knew the overwhelming joy that filled the winners.

Unfortunately, too few American pros knew what winning a Ryder Cup felt like. We lost at The Belfry in 2002 and got humiliated in 2004 and 2006. In 2008, for the first time, we were underdogs. Now my job as Ryder Cup captain was to create an environment where our guys could bond and thrive as a team—and be standing on the right side of that razor-thin line on Sunday evening.

•

Losing so badly in recent Ryder Cup competition presented me with a great opportunity to make fundamental changes to the well-established system. Had we not gotten our butts kicked in years past, I probably would have met more resistance to my ideas. But as is the case in business or social settings, great challenges open the door for even greater innovation.

I didn't believe I was smarter or more talented than any of the captains who had come before me. If anything, I had less experience than a lot of guys who could have been chosen. I'd never coached anything in my life. At least some of the people in contention had managed Little League teams. My wife, Toni, and I have daughters. We were involved in dance recitals, not baseball games.

If I had anything going for me, it was that the players believed I was on their side. As a broadcaster, I had gone out of my way to make sure the players were the stars. My philosophy in the booth had always been to say less instead of more, to tell the viewer something he didn't already know, and to make the players the heroes. That was why I never predicted a shot. *"I think he might be able to chip that one in, don't you, Roger?"* *"He sure could, Johnny."*—chip shot goes in—*"Great call, Johnny."* *"Thank you, Roger."* I never wanted that to be me. My attitude was, the guy who chipped in deserved the praise, not the guy who predicted it. Players knew that about me, and they knew I was always on their side.

By the time our guys teed off on Friday morning of the 2008 Ryder Cup, every player had confidence in my confidence in him. They also knew they were in control of the outcome. I had control over the selection of some of the players, the pairings, the golf course setup, the uniforms, the meals, the team room, the practice round schedule, and the message I could deliver to our team. But the outcome was up to the players, eight guys who had earned their way into this pressure cooker and four others I had invited to join us. The players were the heroes. They were the guys under the spotlight, the guys who would forever have the won-lost numbers by their names, and the guys who would be remembered for hitting the shots and making the crucial putts. That is exactly the way it should be. The players did it, not the captain or any of his assistants.

I sat in my bright-red cart, knowing these were the greatest golfers in the world. We had done everything we could to create an environment where they could be their best. Our team was as prepared as they could possibly be when the bell rang. And I knew that the guys we had assembled would lay everything on the line for each other.

That's all I could ask.

2

THE POD STRATEGY

$\int$erving as Ryder Cup captain is the one of the greatest honors you can bestow on a professional golfer. After a certain point in your career, the possibility stays in the back of your mind and often becomes a topic of conversation. Remembering our friend Payne Stewart, former Ryder Cup Captain Dave Stockton told *GolfWorld* magazine, "There were four of us. Paul Azinger, Lanny Wadkins and Payne and I were always talking about Ryder Cup stuff. Strategies, what you would do, that kind of stuff." It was always there. Years before the PGA of America asked me to be 2008 Ryder Cup captain, I was considering how I might build and lead the team. Lying on my couch with my shoes off, I sipped sweet iced tea and watched a show about Gibson guitars on the Discovery Channel. When the show ended, I was too lazy to hunt for the

The strategy involved breaking the twelve-man team into four-man pods to facili-
tate better communication and reinforce relationships with the players. Here the
"Aggressive pod," Phil Mickelson, Justin Leonard, Anthony Kim, and Hunter
Mahan, practice together on Thursday. ~ R.B.

remote, so I started watching a documentary on how the navy turns raw recruits into SEALs, the most effective and feared fighting force ever assembled. Between segments on special weapons and tactics training and "drown proofing" the troops, one of the officers explained the strength of these Special Operations Forces. "We break the men into small groups," he said. "That's the core. Those guys eat, sleep, and train together until they know what the others are thinking."

Interesting concept, I thought. *Small groups. Tight bonds.*

I sat up as the officer continued, "Every man knows what his fellow SEAL is going to do before he does it. They bond with each other in a way you can't understand if you've never been there."

"Hmm, that might work," I thought out loud.

Toni had just stepped into the room, and she asked, "What might work?"

"In the Ryder Cup," I said. "We've been trying to get twelve guys to come together as a team, when it might work better to break them into smaller units like the SEALs."

For the better part of two decades, sports fans had wondered why European golfers appeared to gel as a unit when the Ryder Cup rolled around, and Americans seemingly did not. Golf, as a sport, was the same in Spain, Italy, and Lithuania as it was in Seattle, Indiana, and Little Rock. European Tour players were individual athletes in an insular sport. The "team," if there was one in golf, consisted of the player and his caddie. Yet in the Ryder Cup the twelve players on the European team always seemed to meld. They showed up looking like the L.A. Lakers, while some thought the Americans brought twelve individuals wearing matching clothes.

The media speculated it was because the Europeans traveled together and were closer than our guys. That's not true. The U.S. wasn't a twelve-man-twelve-private-jet team, just as the Euros didn't share train cars and hotel rooms. American golfers were friendly with each other off the course and tried to beat each other's brains out on it, just like the Europeans. Golf is not a team sport. That is true on both sides of the Atlantic. If anything, the U.S. players should understand the whole "team" thing better than their European counterparts, because most American pros played on college golf teams.

So why did the Europeans always show up for the Ryder Cup looking like a team that had been playing together for years?

That was the question.

"We've been trying for years to get all twelve guys to come together as a team," I told Toni. "Tour players are hardwired to beat the guys next to them, then one week a year we think they should go against their nature and become a championship team. But maybe twelve is too big. If you want to bring the Ryder Cup team together, maybe you have to break it apart."

Even as I was saying it, I realized the idea was something I had instinctively felt for years. Now it was coming clear. We needed to take the concept of the SEALs and somehow apply it to golf. Military experts knew that in the heat of battle you couldn't get a battalion or a company to gel as a single fighting unit. The numbers were too big. But you could get three, four, five, or maybe as many as six guys to lay everything on the line for the men beside them. Small groups—men who ate, slept, trained, hung out, and sometimes fought together—were a key to military success.

At that moment, I thought it could be the answer to America's Ryder Cup woes as well.

There was a reason some of the teams I had played on and others I had watched from the sidelines hadn't clicked, a reason that had nothing to do with talent or desire. It was as simple as watching kids on a playground, or the players on a baseball team sitting in the dugout, or seeing how parents gathered during intermission at a ballet. It was nothing more complicated than observing basic human nature and watching how people cluster. In any unstructured setting, people gather in small groups: three, four, or maybe five total. Whether you are part of a fifty-man football team, a hundred-piece orchestra, or a twelve-person committee, smaller groups will invariably form within the larger body. In orchestras, they're known as "sections." In high school they're called "cliques." In politics, they're known as "inner circles" or "kitchen cabinets." In churches they are "committees" or "prayer groups." In civic and social settings they're "boards" or "advisory groups," and in business they are "departments" or "teams."

We didn't have small "breakout" groups in the Ryder Cup. Maybe we needed them.

That night, watching the SEALs run obstacle courses and lift wet logs over their heads, I developed the germ of an idea, one that crystallized what I had felt for years about the Ryder Cup. A twelve-man team is too big to manage, especially when you're asking them to bond into a seamless unit in one week—a week that is a pressure cooker like the Ryder Cup. In the heat of battle—in pressure unlike anything else in our game—twelve men simply would not bond as a seamless unit in that short a time. We shouldn't force them to try.

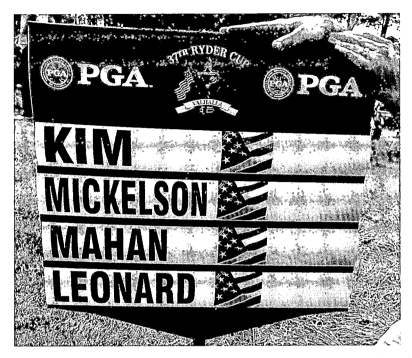

Each pod practiced together all week and barring injury would be paired only with members of their own pod during competitive rounds. A successful corporate model for well-rounded team building involves developing subteams that can aggressively execute a plan, influence others to action, and build quality relationships. Paul was willing to employ this strategy as Ryder Cup captain. ~R.B.

But three men might become like brothers, or even four or six. The exact size of the small groups wasn't as important as the concept. If I became Ryder Cup captain, I knew that I would build a team by breaking it apart into small clusters, or "pods."

•

For the first half-century after seed merchant Samuel Ryder donated the Cup, the matches were held between the United

States and a team from Great Britain and Ireland. The U.S. usually won, and the matches weren't very popular. In the late seventies, when Spaniard Seve Ballesteros hit the scene, Jack Nicklaus proposed expanding the Great Britain and Ireland team to include all of Europe so that players like Seve and Bernhard Langer, from Germany, could compete. Suddenly the matches changed. From 1979, the first year all of Europe competed, through 2007, Europe won eight Ryder Cups; the U.S. only won six. In 1987 Jack got a firsthand taste of what he'd created when Europe beat Team America at Muirfield Village, Jack's course in Dublin, Ohio, 15–13. Not only was it the first time the Americans had lost on U.S. soil, but the captain was none other than Jack Nicklaus. That Ryder Cup also remains historic because it was the only time the teams did not march in for the closing ceremonies. The reason? The U.S. team was sitting in Jack's living room getting their butts chewed out.

Changing from a Great Britain and Ireland to a European team did more than just expand the talent pool. Perhaps the reason the Europeans gelled as a team had nothing to do with the chumminess of the European Tour or the fact that their pros are friendlier than ours. Maybe the reason they won so many Ryder Cup matches had nothing to do with the quality of European golf versus American golf. It could have been that the key to the Europeans' success was the natural inclination to cluster in small groups based on nationalities. José María Olazábal and Seve Ballesteros were the perfect partnership, in part because they had a kinship that went deeper than golf. They were Spaniards, a minority within their own team. So they hung out together, practiced together, ate together, and enjoyed the benefits of a language that their opponents (and many of their teammates) probably didn't speak. The same was true with the Swedes and the Irish. Even the English formed cliques. Faldo had an army of partners over the years, most of them successful, and many of them fellow countrymen. In 2002, the last time I played on a Ryder Cup team, Paul McGinley won the point that sealed the Cup for Europe. But who did McGinley partner with in the foursomes and fourball matches? Padraig Harrington and Darren Clarke, his fellow Irishmen. When Paul Lawrie was a rookie Ryder Cup player, who did Mark James pair him with? Another Scot, Colin Montgomerie. When they did break up into different nationalities, it was usually to pair best friends together like Darren Clarke and Lee Westwood. The makeup of the European team seemed to lend itself to smaller groups. So it could have been that the very nationalism that leads to tensions in other settings had given them a winning edge in the Ryder Cup.

The simple team-building concept I had been thinking about for years, which appeared to be intuitive in most humans yet went largely unnoticed, had been tested, literally, on the battlefield. But I had never seen it consciously applied to golf. That became the reason I felt compelled to try to become the Ryder Cup captain in the first place.

Yet I had to ask if I really wanted the captaincy. I'd seen the demands that are required of Ryder Cup captains, and I'd heard the criticisms leveled at past captains. I'd seen good men—people like Tom Kite, Curtis Strange, Lanny Wadkins, and Hal Sutton—get pummeled in the press when America didn't win. All those guys did was contribute two years of their lives to promoting and preparing for three days of golf where they had no control over a single shot. Sure, you could disagree with some of the decisions those captains made, but the browbeating they took was so out of proportion that it made me wonder if it was worth it.

Then, when Nick Faldo was named captain of the 2008 European team, I felt I was a logical pick to head the American side.

Nick and I were known as fierce combatants on the course and the odd couple in the ABC broadcasting booth we had shared for two years. If the PGA of America wanted to showcase their event to the broadest possible audience, picking me to go up against Faldo made sense, but it wasn't a lock. I wasn't assured of being asked to be captain.

That thought caused my competitive instincts to kick in, and I lobbied for the job as hard as I could, calling every PGA of America official I knew and selling myself as the right man.

That's when my wife, Toni, stepped in and said, "Paul, are you lobbying for a job you want, or are you being the girl who's offended that she hasn't been asked to the prom?"

I had to think about that for a second. Then I replied, "No, I want to be the captain."

Then she asked the most important question of all: "Why?"

I forced myself not to blurt out the first canned answer that popped into my head—some cliché like, "I think I can make a difference," or "It's a wonderful opportunity to represent my country." Even if true, those answers didn't get to the crux of what Toni was asking. She wanted to know what was driving me, what internal mechanism was pushing me to want this.

After letting the question linger for a while, Toni said, "Well?"

The rivalry between Paul and Nick Faldo during their playing career, in the broadcast booth, and as Ryder Cup captains would become an interesting sub-plot. Hunter Mahan would say later, "We knew how badly Paul wanted to beat Nick Faldo, but he never said it to us. He didn't want it to be about him and Nick." In sports competition, controlled tension often creates positive momentum and offers a greater focus for the team. ~ R.B.

I paused and thought for yet another second. Finally I articulated what had been running through my mind for years. "I have a responsibility to try to turn this thing around—a responsibility to the players. I want to create the best possible environment for them, and I think I can do that. I have an idea, a concept, for how to structure the team so that it gives us the best chance possible to succeed. I don't think I'd be able to live with myself if I didn't try."

In October 2007 I met with officials of the PGA of America, which is when the sales job really began. We gathered at a restaurant in Orlando for a steak dinner. It was the week of the tour event at Disney, and I felt certain that this was my interview for the captaincy. PGA of America CEO Joe Steranka was there, along with the PGA president, Roger Warren; vice president, Jim Remy; and the director of media and communications, a smart and talented guy named Julius Mason. We talked for a while about various golf-related things until finally the subject of the Ryder Cup came up. That's when I laid the seeds of my idea out for them.

"By breaking the larger team into smaller units, either three four-man teams or four three-man teams, not only can we get these guys to become closer, we can give them a system that they understand," I explained to the group. "That's the way the navy builds SEAL teams. Those guys might go out as a sixteen-man group to destroy a terrorist training camp or something, but once they're in the field, they break out into small groups of four or five guys—people they've been eating, sleeping, and training beside—so that they know exactly what's coming from the man next to them. Once the mission is complete, they come back together as a larger group."

I didn't know if sharing this was helping or hurting my cause in terms of being asked to be captain, but I believed that breaking the team into small units was the key to giving America the best possible chance at victory, so I didn't hold back. "If I tell our players on the front end, 'Here are the two or three people you're going to play with all week,' that will be a relief to them. They'll play all their practice rounds together and there won't be any surprises."

That was a big and important change. There were times in past Ryder Cups when I was paired with guys that I didn't have a lot in common with. Sometimes I was paired with guys that I hadn't played with in a single practice round. When that happened, we spent the first quarter of our match feeling each other out, and by then we were usually down and trying to claw our way back. By dividing the team into pods, I thought the players would be more comfortable from the first tee on.

Everyone at the table seemed intrigued by what I was saying. Roger Warren was particularly interested. A former basketball coach, Roger and I had spoken prior to this dinner. I'd given him some broad outlines of what I had in mind, and he said he loved the idea. By the time the dinner was over, Roger said, "Well, Zinger, we came here expecting to ask you to be the 2008 Ryder Cup captain, and you haven't said anything tonight to dissuade us from that decision. So would you like to captain the team?"

I said, "I came here tonight hoping you would ask, and thinking I would ask for a few days to think about it. But what the heck, I'll say yes right now, but it's conditional on one thing. I want to change the selection process."

"What do you have in mind?" Roger asked.

I gave them a brief outline, and we all agreed to meet again two weeks later. I knew I still had a lot of coalitions to build.

•

I was convinced I had stumbled onto something, but I knew I still had a lot to learn. So I continued to solicit ideas from as many discreet sources as possible. The last thing I wanted was for the press (and by extension, our European opponents) to get wind of what I was thinking, so I prefaced conversations by saying, "Look, I've got this idea, but it's just an idea at this point, and I want your opinion, but you have to promise not to tell anybody, because I don't want it to get out."

This allowed me to keep my pod idea a secret until after the matches, and in the meantime I brought trusted people into a small circle. I wasn't dictating my plan to them; I was letting them in on a secret, asking their opinions, and swearing them to silence. They became owners of the plan with me and freely offered advice as we moved forward. I remember Ronald Reagan once saying, "There is no limit to what a man can do or where he can go if he doesn't mind who gets the credit." So rather than "tell" people what I intended to do with the Ryder Cup team, I called some past Ryder Cup captains, and people who may or may not have known what the job entailed, and said, "Look, I've got this idea, and I'd love to know what you think about it." To a man, they encouraged me to keep developing the idea. Yes, it was different, and several people responded with things like, "Wow, that's out there," but nobody thought it was terrible or dumb. Everyone agreed we needed to try new things, and this idea was certainly new. Over time I built a groundswell of support among important people within the game without divulging too much.

Then I invited all the former captains to a dinner to talk about the Ryder Cup. Raymond Floyd, Lee Trevino, Ben Crenshaw, Lanny Wadkins, Tom Kite, Hal Sutton, Tom Lehman, Dow Finsterwald, Billy Casper, and Jack Burke Jr. attended. We sat in a private room, and I asked each of them to share their thoughts and feelings about what we needed to do to turn our fortunes around. Everyone had strong opinions. One captain thought our guys didn't take the event seriously enough. He believed that the next captain needed to take a hard-line approach. Another thought the Ryder Cup had lost some of its luster and that today's players had no appreciation for the history of the event. He thought the next captain needed to emphasize the chance to make history. The passion was palpable. These men loved the Ryder Cup and wanted nothing more than for Americans to turn this ship around. Each captain had a slightly different idea of how that should be accomplished.

After listening to everyone and making notes of their suggestions, I told them what I had been thinking. When I laid out the idea of the pod system, the room fell into silence. Finally I heard a couple of guys in the back of the room say, "Wow!" I think it was a good "wow." Then Raymond Floyd, whom I would later name as an assistant captain, stood up and said, "That's a heck of an idea. I don't know if what you're talking about will work. But what I do know is, given how we've performed recently, we need something different, and this is definitely different."

When the dinner adjourned, I felt like I had built a coalition of captain-advocates, a group of veterans who would support my ideas as we marched forward. Developing that kind of support was critical. These were not minor tweaks I was talking about. This was a wholesale change in the way America approached the Ryder Cup, and wholesale changes do not become successes by fiat. They require broad-based support. I would spend the better part of two years building allies.

•

Players were also fascinated. Later, I shared the idea with Jim Furyk. I called him and said, "Jim, I want to describe something to you, and I just want you to listen for a few minutes until I'm finished. Then I want to know what you think." I filled Jim in, and he was fully engaged.

The next day Jim called me and said, "I can't stop thinking about your idea. I couldn't wait to get off the course to talk more about it."

Jim was already talking about how to structure the pods and who would fit best with whom. That made me breathe a little easier. It was one thing to have former captains and PGA of America officials tell me they liked the idea, but none of them would be on the team. When a player gave his seal of approval, I felt a lot better about where we were headed.

I also explained the idea to Tiger Woods. As the number-one player in the world, I assumed Tiger would be a critical leader on the team. Having him on my side from the beginning was more than a little important. When I explained the pod system to Tiger, I said, "I haven't decided on the size of the pods yet. It might be two pods of six players each, or four pods of three players each, or three pods of four players each."

"Four players," Tiger said without hesitation. "It's got to be four."

"Why four?" I asked.

He shrugged. "It's the perfect number."

I mulled that over for a while before mentioning it to anyone else, and I didn't immediately commit myself to the four-man pods. But the more I thought about how to structure the teams, the more this idea made sense. When I talked to Phil Mickelson about what I was thinking, I went through the same conversation I'd had with Tiger. Phil had a similar reaction, but with more specific reasons.

"If you're undecided, I'd say go with four-man units," he said.

"That's what Tiger said," I replied. "Why four?"

"That way if everybody in a group is playing well, you don't have to sit anybody," he said. "If you're committed to everybody playing inside their smaller groups, and each unit has three men, you have to sit somebody in the fourball and foursome matches no matter how well they're playing. With four, everybody can play."

Four, indeed, was the best way to go.

The big thing, the idea that would serve as the foundation for the other team-building principles we would use, was bonding the team by breaking it apart into smaller units. It was a universal principle that some successful organizations did intentionally, and some did by accident. But as I discovered throughout this process and through observation, the power of smaller groups applies everywhere that humans interact. I hoped we could make it work to our advantage in the Ryder Cup.

3

STARTING WITH GREAT

*A*t my dinner with the past captains, Dow Finsterwald, a former PGA champion and a wonderful eighty-year-old gentleman, told a story. "There was a fighter," Dow said. "Before every bout, he would kneel in his corner and make the sign of the cross before the bell rang. Well, he won one fight, and then another and another, and finally somebody asked him, 'Son, do you think making the sign of the cross helps you?' The boy said, 'Yes, sir, I do, but it also helps if you can fight.'"

That was a great story with an important message. A plan was good. A strategy was prudent. But if you couldn't fight, you were probably going to lose. I understood that unless our Ryder Cup team showed up in Louisville with the best players—guys who knew how to win and who were playing at the tops of their games—none of the things I did as captain would matter. As I

Any system, no matter how effective, requires execution from great players like Jim Furyk to ensure success. ~ R.B.

have told numerous business groups afterward, "I had a team-building plan, and a messaging strategy that I thought would help us win the Ryder Cup. But I also had twelve of the best players in the game. If I'd shown up with a bunch of amateurs, all the planning in the world wouldn't have mattered. Europe would have kicked our butts."

I knew we had to field a team that gave us the best possible chance, which meant revamping the qualifying and selection process. I made that case in my second meeting with PGA of America officials at their offices in Palm Beach Gardens, Florida.

The PGA offices sit in a glass building with a marble lobby, a sweeping postmodern staircase, and a lot of hallways with offices featuring full-wall windows overlooking PGA National Resort. It reminded me of some of the government buildings I'd seen in Washington, D.C.—not the classic old architecture like the White House or the Smithsonian but contemporary stuff like the IRS building or the EEOC. The people who work there are wonderful, but the setting, with the sun pounding through the plate glass, didn't do a lot to alleviate my nervousness as I prepared for the most important sales pitch of my life.

I was asking for three changes in the Ryder Cup qualification and selection system: limit the time period for qualifying to one year instead of two; base the qualifying on money earned rather than top-ten finishes; and give the captain four picks instead of two.

My first request was for the time period for qualifying, eliminating the "off" year when the Ryder Cup wasn't played. Everybody thought about the Ryder Cup during the Ryder Cup year, but not the year before. Awarding points for finishing tenth in an event twenty months before the matches didn't make sense. So I floated what would turn out to be one of the most controversial proposals of my early tenure.

"I think we should only count events in the year the Ryder Cup is played," I began after we sat down at the conference table.

That was a huge change I was proposing. As long as there had been qualifying criteria for making the Ryder Cup team, it had encompassed two seasons. There had been various tweaks over the years—points earned in the year of the matches counting more than those in the off year, that sort of thing—but nobody had ever proposed dropping the off year entirely.

I knew we needed to take the hottest players in the game at the time of the matches, and the system as it stood did not necessarily recognize those people. If a player won five times in the off year, he could be playing terrible by the time of the matches and still make the team. I knew. I had been there.

Most people had no idea how badly I was hitting the ball when I arrived at the 2002 Ryder Cup in England. The year before, in 2001 when we were originally scheduled to play, I was playing great. But the 9/11 attacks delayed the matches for a year, and in twelve months I went from contending in majors to having every shot clank like a dropped bag of nickels. Things were so bad that at The Belfry prior to the matches, I sought help from the opposition—in this case, Bob Torrence, an old friend and legendary teacher who also happened to be the father of the European captain that year, Sam Torrence.

I'd known Bob for years. European Tour players from far and wide traveled to his driving range in Scotland, a place with no heated bays, no video equipment, and threadbare mats. Bob's genius made it worth it. He was a master teacher. So when he wandered onto the range during one of the practice days, I didn't hesitate to say, "Bob, would you mind looking at my swing. I'm hitting it awful."

In a gravelly Scottish brogue so thick I could barely understand him, he replied, "Zinger, A'll 'ave a look ot ye, boot you canna tell Sammy. He mayt kill me, or werce, tell me wife."

"No, I won't tell Sam," I promised.

After watching a few swings, Bob said, "Zinger, Ben Hogan unce tole me the secret o' golf, an' if ye promise notta tell Sammy, A'll tell ye."

"Yeah, of course, tell me!" I said. Ben Hogan secrets were the holy grail of golf, even to tour pros.

"O'gay," Bob said, "Hogan said, kee' nu ha mmb an' nare klo ba' ng hit. An' 'at's the secret o' golf."

Before I could say, "Sorry, I didn't catch that," the European squad showed up, and Bob left to join his team. My only chance of learning Hogan's secret of golf was lost in translation, just like my golf game during that Ryder Cup.

Still, fans couldn't tell how much I was struggling. Most amateurs would have killed to hit the ball the way I did that week. Pros knew though. Captain Curtis Strange played me in only one team match, one that Tiger and I lost, and I had to hole a bunker shot at eighteen on Sunday afternoon to halve my singles match against Niclas Fasth, a match where I was grinding all day.

I didn't want to go to Louisville with anyone who was swinging the way I had at The Belfry. We needed every player on the team to be at the top of his game. To accomplish that, I thought we needed to only count events in the year of the Ryder Cup toward qualification.

There was some pushback, as I expected. One PGA official said, "Whoa, we can't just eliminate a year of qualifying."

"Why not?" I asked. The only way to change outcomes is to change events. The definition of insanity is doing the same thing over and over again and expecting a different result. We had been doing things one way for years and we'd been losing. I was doing more than proposing a change in qualifying; I was challenging orthodoxy. If we were using a two-year qualification system "because that's how it's always been done," then we needed to try something different, because what we'd done hadn't worked too well.

Joe Steranka, a thoughtful and reasoned CEO, came up with a logical rationale for keeping at least some of the two-year qualification program. "Yes, you want a player who's hot, but you also want somebody who's consistent, and that's what a two-year system gives you," he said. "We've weighted it so tournaments in Ryder Cup years have more of an impact."

Joe also made another interesting point, one I'd never considered. "We want people thinking about the Ryder Cup in off years," he said. "Yes, it isn't the top priority for a lot of players, but you don't want them to completely forget about the Ryder Cup."

"Fair enough," I agreed. "But we need to do something to move more of the qualifying to the year of the matches."

Another PGA official suggested we just count the majors in the off years. Everybody on the team would likely be playing in the majors, and those are the most important events of the year, so why not add to their value by making them the only four events where you earn Ryder Cup points in the off year.

I liked that idea. It was a good compromise and a great way to confirm the importance of the Masters, the U.S. Open, the British Open, and the PGA Championship. Those four events would become benchmarks for Ryder Cup qualification in the off year.

It was a good thing the PGA Tour commissioner wasn't in that meeting. The tour and the PGA of America call themselves "sister" organizations, but a lot of golf fans and even some journalists don't understand the difference; they just lump everybody together as "the PGA." They are different organizations located in different cities with vastly different priorities. The PGA Tour runs most of the golf tournaments you see on television every week. The PGA of America is made up of golf professionals working at clubs throughout the country. They are the guys giving lessons, running member-guest tournaments, and selling equipment and apparel, and their organization runs two tournaments the general public knows: the PGA Championship and the Ryder Cup. Unfortunately the PGA Tour doesn't run any of the four majors. They have tried for years to position the Players Championship, a fine event held at the TPC at Sawgrass in Florida every year, as a major event, but it has never broken the barrier. I knew the tour would be upset that we were, in essence, cutting them out of an entire year of Ryder Cup qualifying while validating the importance of the four majors, but it couldn't be helped. The "majors only" compromise for the off year was a great decision, and one that ultimately proved successful. I had no intention of disrespecting the tour—on the contrary, I was living a lifestyle I would have never dreamed possible because of the visionary success of the PGA Tour—but I had to build a team of fighters, and this was the best way to do it. The pressure that you feel in major championships is much greater than it is in regular tour events. If we were going to whittle down the tournaments that counted toward Ryder Cup qualification, it only seemed right that we stick with the four that meant the most to the players.

The second change I proposed to the assembled PGA of America officials was to eliminate the top-ten points system. Under the qualifying system in place at the time, players earned points for finishing in the top ten of a tournament. You got bonus points for a win and more points in the majors. The points doubled in the year of the Ryder Cup so as to reward players who had high finishes closer to the time of the matches.

"This system made perfect sense back when 99 percent of the players on the PGA Tour were American," I explained. "I mean, you had Gary Player and Bob Charles, but prior to Greg Norman, that was about it. Now you can look down the leaderboard any given week, and in addition to the Europeans, you'll see guys from Korea, Japan, Fiji, Australia, South Africa, New Zealand, Colombia, and Argentina. The top four Americans any given week might finish fourth, eleventh, twelfth, and fifteenth. Under the current system only one of those guys earns Ryder Cup points. That's got to change."

Most of the PGA officials were nodding before I finished.

"I only choked for two things," I said, "cash and prestige. If I had a chance to win a prestigious event, the butterflies showed up. If I didn't have a chance to win, but had a ten-footer to finish third alone instead of in a four-way tie for third, that was pressure, because that's a lot of money. We have to reward these guys based on the things that matter to them. We have to structure the system to reward prestige and money."

From many players' perspective there were a couple of clear benchmarks on tour: wins and the money title. I thought we should go back to that system as a determinant for making the Ryder Cup. After a lengthy explanation and an hour or so of debate, everyone in the meeting agreed.

"Finally, I said, I want four captain's picks instead of two."

This was the most visible and dramatic change I had proposed so far, but I felt strongly about its importance. In the past, ten men qualified for the team based on the points system, and the captain rounded out the squad with two at-large or captain's picks.

"College coaches recruit all their own players," I continued as I made this pitch. "Pro teams draft or trade for the players they want. That's what creates a team bond. Even a guy sitting on the bench knows the coaching staff wants him. If you want to create loyalty and unity, you have to let the captain pick more of his own players."

What I didn't say was that one of the reasons for wanting more picks was my pod concept. At the time I still wasn't sure if we would go with four three-man pods or three four-man pods. Either way, I wanted at least one pick per pod. Erring on the side of enough picks seemed prudent, so I decided to go for it and ask for four picks.

"That's what I want with the Ryder Cup team," I said. "I want a third of the team to know they are there for no other reason than we believed in them and wanted them there."

Paul sought advice and approval for changes to the Ryder Cup team selection from PGA of America leaders like CEO Joe Steranka. By increasing the number of picks, the PGA leadership gave Paul not only the responsibility of being captain but the authority of leading the team as he saw fit. ~ R.B.

I saw a few big gulps, but in the end, the PGA officials and I reached an agreement on the changes.

•

Once I was comfortable that the selection process would give us the best possible players, I knew it was only the beginning. Without great players, we had no chance regardless of the system; yet having great players was not the end but the beginning. If great skill alone ruled the day, the New York Yankees would win the World Series every year and the Tampa Bay Rays would have no chance. In reality, the Yankees don't win all the time, and a team like the Rays can come out of nowhere and win it all, because having great players is the starting line, not the finish line. You can't win without skill, but greatness alone won't get it done either.

We had to start from great and build accordingly.

If I could get the greatest golfers in the world to buy into the system, I felt we had a chance to make history. There were a few golfers who were obviously going to make the team. Even if they had a ho-hum year, Tiger Woods, Phil Mickelson, and Jim Furyk would qualify. They're that good. Likewise, Stewart Cink would have had to fall off the earth not to earn a spot on the team. Jim is the ultimate grinder, someone who digs a good game out of the dirt. Even when he struggles, he works harder than anybody to get the most out of his game. I was also impressed with the play of young Anthony Kim. He was extremely confident and he had mad skills. Beyond that, much of the team was a question mark.

The 2007 majors proved one of my points. Of the top-ten finishers in the Masters, two were South African, one was English, one was Australian, and one was Irish. The winner, Zach Johnson, was American, but he would be the only American to win a major that year. The U.S. Open was won by an Argentine who had to give his acceptance speech in Spanish. In the top twenty you had a German, a Tobagonian, a Swede, an Australian, a South African, a Canadian, and three Englishmen. The same was true in the British Open, which was won by an Irishman, Padraig Harrington, a great guy and another classic grinder who always got the most out of his game. Only four out of the top-ten players were American. And in the PGA Championship, an Australian and two

South Africans finished in the top ten.

By the beginning of 2008 even the skeptics were breathing a sigh of relief that we had changed the qualifying criteria. However, the team was still like particles in vapor, some defined and some unfocused and unformed. But I felt good knowing I had the ultimate heavyweight champ, the number-one player in the world, Tiger Woods, on my side. Plans, strategies, qualification points, and captain's picks aside, with Tiger I knew I had somebody who could fight.

4

CREATING
THE ENVIRONMENT

$\mathcal{S}$oon after I was named captain, I began to surround myself with people who could help me. For example, I brought in my friend Olin Browne early on to be one of my assistants. Olin was a winner, and I knew the players liked and respected him. I also knew I could rely on his advice. Late in 2007 I named my other two assistant captains, both of whom were former captains themselves: Raymond Floyd and Dave Stockton.

Raymond had captained the 1989 team at The Belfry, and Dave was the captain in 1991 when Raymond and I both played on the team. Asking them to be assistants defied all conventional wisdom. In the past everyone thought assistant captains needed to be active on the tour and close to the guys on the team, or at least peers who might have logged a round or two with a few of the players. I had

Two of Paul's assistant captains, Dave Stockton and Raymond Floyd, were former Ryder Cup captains themselves. Their years of experience and wisdom made it easier for Paul to share leadership responsibilities within the pods. ~ R.B.

different thoughts. Rather than focus on whether or not an assistant captain had played a couple of rounds with one of the guys on the team, I needed men who would reinforce our message and help me keep tabs on how everyone was feeling and playing. Raymond and Dave fit that bill. They were respected by everyone who would be on the team. Even if the players didn't know them well, I knew they would enjoy getting to know them. Plus, I had three assistants for a reason: one assistant for each pod.

Choosing Olin, Raymond, and Dave also sent a clear message: I was going to surround myself with the best people I could. Dave was a former PGA champion who had captained the "War by the Shore" when the U.S. won the Ryder Cup on Kiawah Island. And he was one of the most respected short-game specialists in the world. Raymond was a Hall of Fame legend who had won four major championships, and like Dave, had captained a Ryder Cup team. I'm sure some people thought that asking them to be my assistants showed a lack of confidence in my own abilities, but actually the opposite was true. I didn't care about appearances or conventional wisdom. If I had thought it would have helped us win, I would have asked every living former captain to come on board. I asked Raymond and Dave because I had played with them and for them, and I knew their style. I also knew they believed in my plan and would do whatever it took to make it work.

When the choice of Raymond and Dave became public at the 2007 PGA Championship, one of the first questions I got was from a British reporter, who articulated what others might have been thinking. "Paul," he asked in a distinct public school accent, "does picking former captains like Raymond Floyd and Dave Stockton in

Delegating responsibilities to assistant captain Olin Browne, his good friend and fellow touring professional, freed Paul to make quick responses to situations as they developed on the course. ~ R.B.

any way signal a lack of confidence in your own leadership ability?"

I answered, "I suppose you could look at it that way, but you could also draw the opposite conclusion: that I am confident enough in my own leadership to surround myself with strong leaders."

That was the message I wanted to send to the public and to the players. We would create a culture of confidence that permeated every level of our team. Asking Raymond, Dave, and Olin to be my assistants was one big step in building that culture.

I never once worried that Raymond or Dave would do anything to usurp my leadership. They were far too professional for any of those games. Their goals were to support me and our team and help us win. I had confidence in them, and they had confidence in me. I knew they would be sold out for the team.

From the outset, I did whatever I could to build our culture of confidence while communicating our goal and our role in the public arena. From the moment I accepted the job of captain until the matches were complete, I was the guy responsible for the message. One of the great mysteries to golf fans is what the Ryder Cup captain does in the many months before the matches take place. Even aficionados tend to think it's a matter of picking shirt patterns, making captain's picks, and then showing up with the team *without* your clubs. I learned pretty quickly that it is much, much more. Having been on past teams, I had an idea that there were a lot of things the captain had to deal with, and how crazy the job could become. What I didn't appreciate was just how important every word I uttered in those two years would be. The day I was officially introduced as the 2008 captain, I had a dozen media interviews. In the weeks following, I was on radio and television talk shows, I gave print interviews, and I talked a lot to Internet media. Even though the requests slowed down, I must have averaged an interview a day for two years.

That's when I realized how critical my early role would be in setting the tone for these matches. Any time you have a pulpit for an extended period of time, you have an opportunity to mold perception and steer the public's image of your event. That's not something I always understood as a player, but once I went into the broadcast booth, it didn't take long to figure it out.

When I signed on to be the booth analyst for ABC alongside Nick Faldo, I realized I would develop an on-air character. That's not to say I was disingenuous in the booth—far from it. The camera doesn't lie and a phony can be spotted in no time, especially when he's on air as many hours as we were. But if you watched those broadcasts, you probably noticed the banter. If someone left a putt six inches short, I might say something like, "Nick, you ever wonder what would happen if he'd started just six inches closer to the tee markers?" That gave Nick the chance to say, "No, nobody thinks quite like you, Zinger." I purposely teed Nick up so he could make cracks like that. Occasionally that was my role.

My role as Ryder Cup captain was to create the best environment for our team to play at their highest level. That role included delivering the right message. At press conferences I talked about what a big job we had ahead of us, how the Europeans had dominated the event, and that no matter who made the team we would probably be the underdogs. I worked very hard to craft a message that said, "We're going to do everything we can to prepare hard and we're going to give it everything we have." But I also embraced the role of the underdog. The message I sent was intended to influence people and bring them onto our side while eliminating the pressure from our guys.

During that process, I also had to work through the information the PGA of America provided for me. I was stunned by the volume of documents, although in hindsight it made sense. The PGA had been managing Ryder Cups since 1927. For each new captain, it was a new experience. The organization knew all the pitfalls and details that the captains did not, so they basically gave me a point-by-point list of everything that needed to happen prior to the matches, and everything that would happen once we got to Louisville. Sifting through that information and tailoring it to our needs took a lot of time, but it was an important piece of the puzzle. Creating a winning environment means getting every little detail right.

●

Throughout the preparatory process, I always had the crutch of the number-one player in the world to lean my worries against when I needed a mental break. Yes, he was only one player, and he had only been on one winning Ryder Cup team in five appearances, but having Tiger Woods on your side was certainly better than not having him.

Like most golf fans, I watched in something resembling awe when Tiger holed a twelve-foot putt on the seventy-second hole of the U.S. Open at Torrey Pines to tie Rocco Mediate, and I sat spellbound the next day as he went on to win the play-off. There was no doubt early in the summer of 2008 that when it came to executing golf shots under pressure, Tiger had no equal. Adding to the drama of that tournament was the obvious pain that Tiger was going through as he struggled around the course on one good knee.

It was one of the few times I had seen Tiger let his pain show on the golf course. For me, one of the most impressive things about Tiger had been his ability to create a persona and maintain that from the moment he arrived at the golf course until the second he left. From the red shirts on Sundays, to the intimidating stares, to the dramatic fist pumps, to his guarded interviews—I mean, really, how many times did the guy say, "It's right there in front of you," or "I'm just trying to be there in the end"?—Tiger never broke character. Other players knew very little about him, and the media knew less. Few hung out with him or worked out with him; only a handful of people knew where he stayed or where he ate.

As I watched him play through his pain at the U.S. Open, I was a little concerned, but I didn't think it was too serious. He had just come back from knee surgery where doctors had shaved excess cartilage from his meniscus. Everybody's sore after surgery. It takes a while to get back to full speed. I figured Tiger needed a week or two of rest and he would be as good as new. And the Ryder Cup was still three months away. Two days later, however, I got the news that he was undergoing major reconstructive knee surgery and would be out for the rest of the year, including the Ryder Cup.

Paraphrasing author and poet Samuel Johnson, Winston Churchill once said, "Nothing focuses your attention like the prospect of facing a firing squad at dawn." He had a good point. There is no doubt that an impending crisis, even one that is far less dire than being shot, heightens the senses and sharpens the mind. If you've ever been in a speeding automobile when an animal runs out in the street, you know what I mean. Your mind zeroes in on the escape line, and your eyesight and fine motor skills become almost supernatural. The prospect of imminent disaster jolts your reflexes into action, and you do things that you never thought possible. Tales of petite women lifting cars to free trapped children are common, and soldiers coming back from combat tell amazing stories of extraordinary eyesight, hearing, and superhuman strength and endurance.

Tiger's knee injury wasn't the equivalent of combat, or rescuing a trapped child, or hitting a deer at seventy miles an hour, but it was a blow to the American Ryder Cup team. Any time you lose the number-one player in the world, maybe the greatest player in history, it's hard to look at it as anything but a setback.

I took a few minutes to process the news before accepting that Tiger would not be on my team. I have learned through my life experiences that you can't control the circumstances that are thrown your way. In fact, all you can control is how you react and respond to those conditions. In his best-selling book, *Man's Search for Meaning*, Auschwitz survivor Dr. Viktor Frankl wrote, "Everything can be taken from a man but one thing: the last of the human freedoms—to choose one's attitude in any given set of circumstances, to choose one's own way."

Tiger was out. I would be going into the Ryder Cup without him. That was not a situation I caused, nor was it something I could control. The only thing I could control was my attitude toward the situation as it was presented. I could control my response, and hopefully, the attitude and response of the team.

How do you turn a challenge like losing Tiger into an opportunity?

I found the answer to be simple: you adapt. You change with the currents and modify the plan to fit the seas that surround you. I couldn't let Tiger's injury and absence distract us. My culture of confidence could not be shattered by the absence of one man.

So I used Tiger's injury as a chance to play up our underdog status in the hopes that fans, media, and particularly our opponents would underestimate us, and it just might take pressure off our team.

•

Lou Holtz, a legendary college football coach and a man I've always admired, was masterful at making the most patsy opponent sound like a contender for the national championship. If Notre Dame was playing a team that hadn't won a game, Lou would figure out a way to make it sound like the Irish were in for the fight of their lives. After a while it became comical, but Lou never broke character. He always played up his opponent and made it sound like his teams had no shot.

With or without Tiger we were going to enter the 2008 Ryder Cup as underdogs. You don't lose as many as we had lost by the margins we had lost them and show up as the favorite. With Tiger we were supposed to lose. Without him, we were expected to lose.

I couldn't change any of that, but I could spin the situation to our advantage by downplaying expectations and encouraging others to underestimate our chances. Not only would this take a lot of pressure off our guys and allow them to relax, freewheel, and enjoy the experience, but I also figured it might unnerve the Europeans.

The hardest game to win is the one you're supposed to win. If I could play up the Europeans as favorites, then maybe they would feel the kind of pressure that our team had been feeling for most of the last quarter century. Our guys could embrace their underdog status and ready themselves for their roles as giant killers.

5

RELATIONSHIPS
TRUMP ASSETS

*D*r. Ron Braund got his professional start as a licensed family therapist and corporate team-building specialist, meaning he had seen almost every compatibility problem imaginable. But prior to that, he was a college basketball player, an undersized point guard who had to win with his mind as much as his skills. "My specialty was in passing and setting up teammates with assists," Ron said. "I would rather make a good assist than score. That characterizes my career approach to counseling, consulting, and team building."

It was also one of the reasons I asked him to help me as we were preparing for the Ryder Cup. At a dinner at Vini Vidi Vici in Atlanta, Ron agreed to give me advice and provide some fresh perspectives on team building. I had twenty-five years experience in professional golf, and Ron had thirty years experience in corporate team building and

Pairing players by compatible personalities was determined to be an important factor to create the best environment for success. Boo Weekley and J.B. Holmes were a great combination in addition to sharing a common Southern heritage. ~ R.B.

relationship development, and had studied and written a book about human behavior and group dynamics and another about thinking styles. That combination could be invaluable, especially since I was considering a new team-building approach to the Ryder Cup.

Ron knew very little about the world of professional golf, which was also good. I needed fresh opinions. Many inside the tour community would have preconceived notions about the Ryder Cup and why we were losing so much. It was important to get insights from someone who understood corporate team building, but who only knew the Ryder Cup from a fan perspective.

When I explained my idea of breaking the team into smaller units based on the SEALs strategy, he responded with a possibility I hadn't considered: "Maybe you could organize the team based on behavioral styles."

"What do you mean?" I asked.

"Well, how would you normally pair players for the Ryder Cup?"

I explained that my first thought had been to break the team up based on the strengths of each player's game. For example, I would probably match bombers with great wedge players. Or if I had three guys who hit it really straight off the tee, I'd pair them with solid iron players. And good putters would fit anywhere. Then I'd thought about putting one strong leader in each pod. If I made Tiger the leader of one pod, Phil Mickelson the leader of another, and Jim Furyk the leader of a third, I could surround them with players who would follow their leads. Tiger and Phil were bombers with great short games, so I could surround them with phenomenal iron players. Jim, on the other hand, hadn't missed a fairway since Hurricane Katrina, so I could add a couple of great putters to his pod. No matter what the combination, my thoughts always revolved around bonding players based on their games.

"So what if, in addition to their playing style or particular strengths on the golf course," Ron offered, "you built the pods on personality style?" Then he explained that from his experience most people who share similar personality styles, values, and backgrounds have an easier time adapting quickly in relationships than people who come at life from different points of view. At that point I understood what he meant about like-minded people being more comfortable with each other.

"You might have two guys whose golf games match up perfectly, but if they're different personality types—if they process information differently, if they communicate differently, and if they handle pressure situations differently—then they are less likely to naturally bond," Ron said.

Tiger and Phil might not have been the best pairing because their personalities were so different, but I still believed golf was a much more important barometer for assembling pods than personality assessments.

Ron kept challenging my conventional thinking. "The old adage 'opposites attract' is often true," he continued. "When you're at a party or at dinner or in some harmless social setting, it's enriching to engage people who are different from you. Curiosity and the thrill of experiencing new things can cause us to be attracted to those who are our opposites. But introduce stress to that relationship, and those opposites will respond very differently. One may want to be alone to avoid any conflict, for example, while the other craves social interaction to work out the problem. So as long as life

Paul and I watch from the first hole tee box during the Friday morning foursomes. We operated on the premise that communication would increase when behavioral style was a matching factor, especially under the intense pressure of Ryder Cup competition. ~ R.B.

remains relatively stress free, opposites do attract. But I don't know anyone who lives a stress-free life. Do you?"

I didn't. Even the most comfortable environments could be stressful. Ryder Cup stress was something altogether different. I knew the pressure of those three days and what the players would experience. We could have moments where patience would be in short supply. As captain, I would do what I could to keep the team focused and relaxed, but in the heat of competition, nerves might be raw, and guys would likely have to rely on each other for support.

"You've seen it in the Ryder Cup where pressure situations have isolated guys who were supposed to be playing together," Ron said. "One guy wants to talk it out and his partner goes silent. Those guys deal with stress differently . . . neither of them is right or wrong, but when you put them on the course together under this kind of pressure, they both need a partner who responds to the pressure of the moment in a similar manner."

"But if I put guys whose games mesh—"

"That can work," Ron interrupted, "but personalities can work as well. Maybe better. These are the best golfers in the world. What you can do in addition to that is give them an environment where the stress of the Ryder Cup actually brings them closer together."

"Are you telling me that the Navy SEALs do psychological evaluations on recruits before assigning them to a team?" I asked.

"Yes," Ron said. "Plus, the navy puts SEALs through eighteen months of training. You've got a week. If you had these guys for a year or two, you could message and train them. They would have time to learn how others respond under pressure. You only have a week; you might think about pairing them according to their personalities."

I thought about some of most successful Ryder Cup pairings I'd witnessed. In 2002 Curtis Strange paired Phil Mickelson with David Toms, which at first I thought was odd. On the surface those two players couldn't have been more different. They got along fine, but David is a cautious, methodical, analytical kind of person who considers many possible outcomes before making a decision. When he won the 2001 PGA Championship at the Atlanta Athletic Club, he beat Phil by laying up his approach shot on the final hole a hundred

For over two years, Paul studied team-building strategies that he would use during his tenure as Ryder Cup captain. This included understanding the importance of relational intelligence which maximizes the potential for teamwork. One result was the pairing of Justin Leonard and Hunter Mahan, who finished 2–0–1 playing together. ~ R.B.

yards short of the green, knowing that he could hit a wedge to within fifteen feet and make the par putt to win. Laying up in that situation was the smart, calculated, higher-percentage decision. It showed discipline and confidence, especially since everybody in the gallery and broadcast booth was urging him to go for the green.

Phil, on the other hand, would have probably gone for that green. He's a swashbuckler who is convinced that he can pull off the miraculous shot whenever it's needed. He calculates the odds of success and makes decisions accordingly. To the casual fan he may appear to be going against convention, but he does so with extreme confidence in his ability to do what others consider "impossible." On the surface, Phil and David couldn't have been a more diametrically opposite pairing. But if you dug a little deeper, beyond the obvious differences in their styles, you found that David and Phil had more in common than you might expect. They were both supremely confident but respectful people. They also believed that their confidence was infectious and that they could inspire the guy walking beside them. They both engaged their caddies as partners, and they enjoyed chatting with fellow competitors. It was not uncommon for them to say to the person in their group, "Let's have some fun and make some birdies," or something equally uplifting. Off the course, both were avid football fans with encyclopedic knowledge of players, coaches, records, stats, and schemes, and both did extraordinary work for young people in their communities.

Curtis kept them together for four matches, and they were 2–1–1 as a team, the leading point getters for the U.S. that year. So as odd a couple as they might have seemed, Phil and David were a good example of what Ron was describing.

Then I thought about Seve Ballesteros and José María Olazábal, the most successful pairing in Ryder Cup history by far with an 11–2–2 record as a duo. If you were putting a pairing together based on the complementary strengths of their golf games, you couldn't find a worse combination than Seve and Ollie. Both were among the greatest short-game players in the world, but they could also go an entire round without hitting a tee shot in the fairway. Logic would dictate that you pair great putters who spray their tee shots with someone who drives the ball straight and hits a lot of greens in regulation. One partner's weakness is offset by another's strengths. That was not the case with Seve and Ollie, yet their Ryder Cup history is legendary.

The more I thought about it, the more I realized that the most successful pairings were, indeed, players who had a lot more in common than golf. Arnold Palmer and Gardner Dickinson weren't the perfect teammates based on the strengths of their respective games, but they were a fantastic duo because they got along so well. Jack Nicklaus and Tom Watson were also a great pairing, because, like Mickelson and Toms, they both exuded supreme confidence in everything they did. Lanny Wadkins and Larry Nelson, Tony Jacklin and Peter Oosterhuis—these were all great players, but why were their pairings successful while so many other duos failed?

The answer was staring me right in the face. It was their behavioral styles. After several weeks of consideration, I decided to follow Ron's advice and break the team into pods based primarily on personality. I settled on the personality aspect of the pod system before I settled on the size of the pods, though I still was leaning heavily toward three four-man teams.

There was only one problem: I knew thirty or so guys who might be on the team, but I was no psychologist. I couldn't tell you what kind of thinkers they were, and I certainly had no idea how

Kenny Perry structured his season around his commitment to the Ryder Cup, ensuring that he would be playing in his home state. ~R.B.

they gathered and processed information. I could tell you that Stewart Cink was a quiet, mild-mannered Christian guy who drove his pickup truck to the hardware store and who liked to take his wife and sons to hockey games, but I knew nothing about the thought processes he used to make decisions or how he experienced life and related to others.

The same was true with Kenny Perry, a guy whose commitment to the Ryder Cup I loved. Kenny had made no secret of the fact that he considered this Ryder Cup to be more important than the majors. Making the team and playing for his country in his home state of Kentucky would be the perfect capstone to his career. Kenny was a passionate guy who owned drag racers and a public golf course in Franklin, Kentucky, and when he wasn't on tour, he could either be found in the garage with a wrench in his hand or behind the counter ringing up greens fees and golf balls. But I wasn't sure what inspired and motivated Kenny. I didn't know how he interacted with others in stressful situations. I couldn't tell you if he became quiet and insular when things got tight or if he became a chatterbox. I'd played with him a few times, but I'd never studied his mannerisms or his interplay with others. Beyond being a nice guy whose company I enjoyed, I couldn't tell you much about the depth of his personality.

Anthony Kim, who I had been watching closely for a couple of years, was a different story. AK, as he's known, hit the tour with as much fanfare as talent. A member of the winning 2005 Walker Cup team and an All-American at Oklahoma University, he turned pro in 2006 at age twenty-one and immediately had an impact, finishing second in his debut at the Texas Open, a tournament he entered on a sponsor's exemption. No one had done that since Tiger turned pro in the fall of 1996. That wasn't AK's only comparison to Tiger. He broke into the top hundred in the world in the first five months of his rookie year with ten top-ten finishes, and he had the low final round in the 2007 U.S. Open.

He also ruffled a few feathers. When members of the press asked him how he felt about being the next challenger for Tiger, AK shrugged and said he welcomed it. "I'm not out here to be number two," he said. This was a street kid with talent and confidence to burn. When he won twice in his second year on tour, he proved that the high expectations were not misplaced. This was a kid with tons of talent who felt at home on top of the leaderboard.

AK was also the kind of guy who wore his hat backward and listened to his iPod while hitting balls—a five-foot-ten California-Asian guy who showed up in the gym at OU and trash-talked all comers on the pickup basketball court. He wasn't afraid of anybody or anything. In fact, once it became obvious that he had made the Ryder Cup team, he spent months coming up to me in the locker rooms and driving ranges saying, "Wassup, Cap'n!"

There was no mystery to his personality profile. He was cocky and direct, but he was also the kind of guy who wanted to be handed the ball on the final play with the game on the line. I didn't know the intricacies of a lot of guys, but I had AK figured out.

"I can develop profiles on the players by having them fill out a small set of questions online," Ron suggested.

"No, you can't," I countered.

"Sure, I can. It's not a test in the sense that there are right or wrong answers. They aren't graded. They're subjective questions. They help evaluate how the player thinks and how he relates to others. It'll show what motivates them, how they gather and process information, and how they make decisions."

I said, "No, I mean I can't approach these guys and say, 'Hey, you mind sitting down in front of your computer and taking this test? I'm trying to crawl into your head and develop a personality profile for the Ryder Cup.' We can't do that. I want the pod system to be effective, and I understand what you're saying about assembling it based on personality styles, but I'm not going to ask players to take a test. Can we come up with another way?"

Ron thought about it for several weeks before coming back with plan B. "I think I can put together effective and fairly accurate profiles based on observation," he said. "With your input, and Olin's input, and some help from my sons Rich and Adam observing on the course, we can come up with some good data based on the players' interaction with their caddies, the fans, and other players."

It wasn't a perfect formula, but it was as good as we were going to get. Ron started his profiles by using some tools of his trade, graphs like the DISC and Myers-Briggs personality profiles.

As time progressed and the list began to narrow as more and more players distinguished themselves as potential qualifiers, Ron's profiling techniques evolved. He streamlined the system until we settled on three distinct pods, each based on a personality type:

➤ The first one would be the "dominant/conscientious" pod, which we called the "Aggressive" pod. These were the guys who believed they could take charge of situations and used a systematic approach to solve problems. I didn't know exactly which members of my team would end up in this pod, but Phil Mickelson and Anthony Kim definitely fit the profile.

➤ The next group was what we called the "influencing/relaters." These would be guys who generated enthusiasm and are comfortable interacting with others. Ben Crenshaw, as both a player and a captain, fit this profile. He gets emotional when the national anthem is played at baseball games, and he always has an inspiring word for anyone in need.

DISC PERSONALITY PROFILE

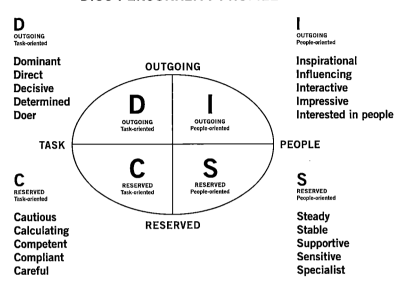

D
OUTGOING
Task-oriented

Dominant
Direct
Decisive
Determined
Doer

I
OUTGOING
People-oriented

Inspirational
Influencing
Interactive
Impressive
Interested in people

TASK

PEOPLE

C
RESERVED
Task-oriented

Cautious
Calculating
Competent
Compliant
Careful

S
RESERVED
People-oriented

Steady
Stable
Supportive
Sensitive
Specialist

MYERS-BRIGGS TYPE INDICATOR

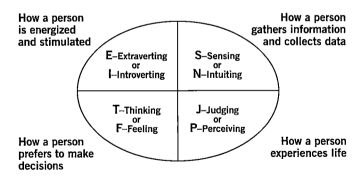

How a person
is energized
and stimulated

How a person
gathers information
and collects data

E–Extraverting
or
I–Introverting

S–Sensing
or
N–Intuiting

T–Thinking
or
F–Feeling

J–Judging
or
P–Perceiving

How a person
prefers to make
decisions

How a person
experiences life

*While observing players on the course at PGA Tour events, I drew upon informa-
tion from two assessment tools used during my career as a licensed therapist and
team builder. These profiles helped to identify personality traits and behavioral
styles for player compatibility. ~ R.B.*

➤ The final subset was my "steady/supportive" pod, or my "Steady Eddies." These would be the unflappable guys, the ones who wouldn't get too high or too low, but who would be the bedrock we would build on when things got heated. I knew Stewart Cink would fit in that group, as would Jim Furyk.

•

We had several players make the team who would have fit in multiple pods. Using various personality assessment criteria, Ron, his colleague and performance consultant Charles Plott, and Olin Browne created an elaborate charting system that showed every possible player combination and suggested which personality styles might be most compatible with one another in competition.

Any pair of Ryder Cup players can win their match on any day. Winning and losing on the golf course is almost always determined by factors other than the personalities of the golfers. But when you're talking about that razor-thin line between winning and losing at the highest level of competition, you look for every edge. As captain I had only so many variables I could control, and pairings were one of them. So if one guy played better with a partner who could fire him up, and another played better with a partner who was less animated, then I was going to give them that. That's what Ron's chart helped me see at a glance. A twelve-man team has sixty-six different possible pairings. The chart labeled each of those potential pairings with either a green light, a yellow caution light, or a red light based on the compatibility of the players' personalities and thinking styles.

I believed in the concept, and soon I would see firsthand from our Ryder Cup experience that great things can be achieved when people with similar personalities communicate and connect on a deeper level, a level that gets at the root of who and what they really are. Yes, at times it seemed subjective, especially to someone like me who hasn't been trained to observe different personalities and how they interact. Boo Weekley would later create the word *compatibate*, which was the perfect made-up word to describe what we hoped to accomplish.

We were planning a major change. And even as confident as I was, I could only pray that it worked.

6

GIVING OWNERSHIP

$\mathcal{A}$s the dog days of summer 2008 hit their stride, our team continued to take shape. In addition to Phil Mickelson, Jim Furyk, Anthony Kim, Kenny Perry, and Stewart Cink, we had some welcome surprises. Boo Weekley was certainly not your typical Ryder Cup qualifier. This was a guy who lassoed alligators from his grandmother's front porch when the river in his native Milton, Florida, rose out of its banks. He wore camouflage hunting wear under his golf shirts in the British Open because it was the warmest stuff he owned. I thought Boo was great for the game. Plus, the guy could really play. When Boo got hot, every iron shot he hit looked like it was going in the hole. He was also somebody who made up words left and right. When the media asked him about me, he said, "Yeah, Cap'n

Steve Stricker was the only captain's pick selected solely by Paul. Steve would have qualified for the team under the previous selection system and was a great personality fit for any of the three pods. ~R.B.

Azinger, he's a real inspirator." I assume that's a combination of *inspiration* and *motivator*, but who knows? It's certainly a Boo-ism, and there would be many more of them during our Ryder Cup experience.

Boo would have fit in any of our pods. He might have believed that I was an "inspirator," but in reality, he was the one who could be counted on to lift his team. Whether it was lightening the team room with stories of boxing with an orangutan, or putting his arm around a teammate and saying, "Let's get 'em," Boo was a serious green light for my "influential" pod.

Another inspirational personality was Kenny Perry. Kenny got choked up talking about the Ryder Cup six months before the matches. In fact, Kenny was so emotionally invested in making the team and playing in his home state that he skipped the British Open. When he qualified for the team in early summer, I called him on the phone, and said, "Kenny, congratulations on your second win. I'm thrilled for you. I know how important this is for you to be on this team and I couldn't be happier."

"Thanks, Zinger," he said. "I'm really excited."

"I know you are, and you're going to want some momentum coming into this thing. There's no reason you can't win once or twice more this year. Keep pushing yourself so you can be ready to shine in September in front of your people."

Kenny did more than that. He won three times in 2008 and had seven top tens, finishing fifth on the money list—the best of his career. And because he and Boo are good ol' boys who feel comfortable in overalls and know their way around a tractor, I fondly nicknamed the grouping my "redneck pod."

We also had Ben Curtis, an Ohio native and former Nationwide Tour player who launched his tour career in 2003 by winning the British Open as a rookie. Ben had his most consistent year on tour in 2008 with five top-ten finishes, including a seventh at the British Open at Royal Birkdale. But it wasn't until he finished tied for second in the PGA Championship (making him low American behind winner Padraig Harrington) that he qualified for the Ryder Cup team. Ben Curtis was about as even-keeled as any player you could find. When he holed an eighteen-footer on the final hole to take the lead in the British Open at Royal St. George's, he waved to the crowd as if he'd just birdied the second hole in the first round. And when he struggled, missing twenty-seven cuts in a two-year stretch, he never showed signs of discouragement. Whether he was winning or going home before the weekend, he gave the impression of being the same steady guy. If you saw him walking down a fairway, you wouldn't know if he was 20-under or 10-over. According to Ron's assessments, that was a classic steady/supporter personality style and fit perfectly into the Steady Eddies pod.

Also qualifying was Justin Leonard, in his first Ryder Cup since making the miracle forty-five-foot putt to clinch the Cup in 1999 and seal the greatest comeback in Ryder Cup history. Justin also had one his most consistent seasons in years with eight top tens in 2008, including a win in Memphis. Not only was he a veteran, but most people knew that Justin had clinched the winning point the last time the U.S. won the Ryder Cup. That was the kind of positive experience we needed.

Justin was one of those players who would have fit in a number of different pods. Not only was he steady, he had a relaxed,

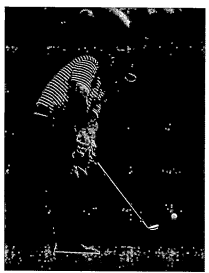

Phil Mickelson

Stewart Cink

Jim Furyk

Kenny Perry

At Paul's request, the PGA of America changed the selection process to place a greater emphasis on performance during the year of the Ryder Cup. The change enabled him to get the hottest players at the right time. These eight made the team following the conclusion of the PGA Championship. ~R.B.

Anthony Kim

Justin Leonard

Ben Curtis

Boo Weekley

easygoing, diplomatic demeanor. He was a calming force and inspired confidence in others around him. That made him a fine complement to the Mickelson-Kim pod. He might not have been the first person who popped to mind when you said, "aggressive," but nobody believed in himself more than Justin. He had to. Justin was not as long off the tee as most guys, and he had to grind out wins through grit, determination, and profound confidence. He could beat anyone, even guys who hit it forty yards longer than him off the tee, and if you had a putt that you needed to clinch the Ryder Cup, who better to hit it than someone who had been there before?

Jim Furyk was as assertive as anyone in the game. He hit the ball straight and had a tremendous short game, but he never seemed to get too up or too down. On the course Jim is totally focused, more reserved in the way he acknowledges the gallery— all the time analyzing his game. When he plays, the next shot is everything. He would have fit nicely with my steady/supportive pod or in the aggressive/conscientious pod with Kim, Mickelson, and Leonard. But I waited before making a final decision on where to put Jim, who had played in five Ryder Cups, because he told me he might like to play with some long hitters.

When qualifying ended the Sunday of the PGA Championship and I had my first eight players, based on the Ryder Cup standings, I called each of them, congratulated them, and filled them in on the ideas for building the team. I told them about watching the SEAL documentary about breaking teams into small groups, and I let each of them know that we had, through observation, done personality profiles on them. This was another critical sales job. I had to get every player who had qualified to embrace our plan. "I want to put you in small groups or units like the SEALs do," I told each of them individually. "Barring injury or illness, I will never take you out of your pod. I want you to strategize together, prepare together, and I want you to sell out completely for the guys in your small group."

Each player had an opinion, and there was discussion back and forth. In the end they were all engaged and on board. For that I was thankful.

Historically the captain made his picks the Monday after the PGA Championship in mid-August. The PGA of America and I changed that, because the Ryder Cup wouldn't be played until late September. Plus, with the way the tour had structured the schedule, several big tournaments were played late in the year. Since golf is a game of streaks, a lot could happen in five weeks' time. If somebody got on a hot streak, I wanted the opportunity to put him on our team.

As time got close, I solicited help. Raymond, Dave, and Olin talked to me extensively about our options, especially after the PGA Championship when only one player stood out. We all agreed that Steve Stricker should be a pick. If the Ryder Cup qualifying time had extended beyond the PGA Championship, Steve's strong finishes in those additional tournaments would have earned him a spot in the top eight. Plus, he was one of the best putters in the world, and a guy who had been Comeback Player of the Year, twice. If heart alone could win it, Stricker was an easy choice. He would have fit in any of the pods, but especially in the steady/supportive pod with Stewart Cink and Ben Curtis.

As I considered the next three captain's selections, I looked back at input I had received over a two-year period from some of my closest friends in the press.

Back when I shared the idea of soliciting input from the media with Julius Mason, the media and communications director for the PGA of America, he was a bit concerned. But I felt passionate about making the media a part of the process. I had been on tour for twenty-five years, and in that time I had developed some trusted relationships with several members of the media. I felt confident asking for their opinions. Who was more plugged in to the players than the guys covering them every week? People might assume that other players know their peers, but that's not always the case. As a general rule, a tour player goes to work, plays his round, hits the range, and heads back to the hotel or the house he's renting. If you get on the wrong side of a draw, you might go an entire season without seeing Phil Mickelson. Even if you win three or four times a year, you might get paired with Phil only once or twice. Guys like Gary Van Sickle from *Sports Illustrated*, Doug Ferguson of the AP, Bob Verde from *Golf Digest*, and Alex Miceli and Tim Roseforte from the Golf Channel saw him every week. A player's job is to play. The media's job is to cover them. I felt it was definitely in our best interest for me to talk to my friends in the press room about potential picks.

When I told Julius about it, he said, "Are you sure you know what you're doing?"

"Trust me," I said. "I'm asking the guys who could rip me to shreds in print to be a part of the process."

I enjoyed reversing roles with them—asking them questions

instead of them asking me. They all had answers, and they all had opinions, and they shared some important information. Alex Miceli, an entrepreneur who started two highly successful golf Web sites and has been a staple in the tour media centers for years, supplied me with reams of statistical data on the top twenty-five players who hadn't qualified. Doug Ferguson, who is out on tour more than most journalists and more than a lot of players, showed me the results of a poll where the media had been asked which players I should pick.

Even with all that data and all those opinions, with the exception of Stricker, no single player jumped off the page. And the tournaments didn't reveal anything; unbelievably, foreigners, including two players from the European team, won six straight beginning two weeks before the PGA Championship and all the way up to Ryder Cup week. Vijay Singh from Fiji won three of the six, Carl Petterson from Sweden won once, Padraig Harrington from Ireland won the PGA Championship, and Camilo Villegas from Colombia won the day before I had to make my picks. As I watched Camilo hole the final putt to win, I turned off the TV and slumped on my couch for a few minutes, wondering what to do. If I was looking for a hot hand, I wasn't finding it among the Americans on the tour.

Finally I called Dave Stockton.

"Who do I pick?" I said. "I have twenty choices and I don't like any of them."

Dave said, "Don't forget your pod system. Don't look at your choices in terms of the overall team; look at them in terms of how they fit in your pods."

Great advice, I thought. We hung up and I walked into my office.

I looked at the eight players who had made the team and quickly came up with four two-man combinations. Knowing I was picking Stricker, I had nine players. After a little jumbling and shuffling around, and several phone calls to players already on the team, I soon came up with three three-man teams. Then I took my list of twenty possible picks whose profiles we had considered, and imagined how each would fit in the system. Just like that, every player on the list made sense. I went from not wanting any of them to wanting all of them, once I saw how and where they fit in our plan. It was at that moment that I knew the pod system was going to work.

I could have picked any of them, but in the end, I didn't pick a single one.

I let the players do it.

That's when I called the guys one more time. I couldn't get Boo. He might have been knee-deep in a swamp hunting hogs, but I reached everybody else. I said, "I'm sorry to bother you again, but we're all in this together now. You're engaged and invested in the process, and I appreciate it. You all have ownership in your pod, but I want to take this one step further. I want to empower you."

To a man they asked, "What do you mean?"

I explained, "You currently have a three-man team. I'm going to give you a list of names that are green lights for your units, and I want you to pick your fourth man. I want you three to get together and fill out your pod. If you decide to pick outside the names that I give you, I'll explain to you why you're wrong. The choices I'm giving you are all playing well, and would all be green lights in your groups."

Other Ryder captains have asked their players for their input. In fact, when Dave Stockton was captaining the 1991 team, he

Hunter Mahan, J.B. Holmes, and Chad Campbell were technically captain's picks. In reality, the players in each of the three pods made the final selections. Paul would often say, "I want the players to have confidence in my confidence in them." When he gave each pod the opportunity to pick the player they wanted, he reinforced self-confidence and raised the level of trust and commitment. ~ R.B.

asked for my feedback on his picks. But I don't know if anyone has ever given the players complete ownership of the captain's picks.

When I told Olin Browne about that decision, he immediately recognized the value of letting the players pick the final man in their pod. "Wow," he said. "What a great way to give them owner-ship of the team. Do Dave and Raymond know?"

"Absolutely," I answered. "We're all in this together now. Now I believe these guys will commit to this plan and go all in."

No one outside the team knew that I let the players pick their own teammates. We kept it a secret until now. The world thought Steve Stricker, Hunter Mahan, Chad Campbell, and J.B. Holmes were my picks, and yes, I was the guy who picked up the phone and asked them to join the team, but Hunter was the choice of Phil

Mickelson, Anthony Kim, and Justin Leonard. Chad Campbell was the consensus pick of Stewart Cink, Ben Curtis, and Steve Stricker. Furyk said, "Give me bombers," and I said, "How 'bout J.B. Holmes?" He loved it. Kenny also loved the idea since he and J.B. were close friends and fellow Kentuckians. J.B. had been an All-American at the University of Kentucky. When I called J.B. and asked him to join us, I heard a quiver in his voice, and I knew he would lay it all on the line in Louisville.

The moment I made the calls, I knew the picks were right. The new guys fit into our plan and were excited about the possibilities. Each of the picks was a solid green light for his respective pod. I also knew that the assistant captains fit into the plan as well. Raymond Floyd would be with the aggressive pod all week—observing them, talking with them, and keeping me informed of their status. Olin fit with Boo, Kenny, Jim, and J.B. He was also someone who could inspire and encourage as well as someone who was in tune with how those guys thought and played. And finally, Dave was as steady as the pod he would be with all week.

•

I was so busy with our team I didn't really start paying attention to the European team until it was time for Nick to make his picks. There was one player who didn't make their team through the standings that I feared more than anyone on their team; Darren Clarke won twice in 2008, including a win the week before Nick made his picks. My stomach ached at the thought that he was surely going to pick Darren Clarke. His emotional leadership on the 2006 team and his successful Ryder Cup history with both Padraig

Harrington and Lee Westwood made him, to me, a stone-cold lock. I felt like he was the hottest player on their tour.

I can't speak for how Nick approached the selection process, but when asked by the press about it, he said, "I've got to go my own way with what I feel it brings to the team. Some will agree, some will disagree, but I'm the guy who has to live with it."

I was wrong in assuming Nick would pick Darren Clarke, and I couldn't have been happier about it. Nick chose two fellow Englishmen, Ian Poulter and Paul Casey, both fine players in their own right.

However, when I heard the news I called Toni and said, "I want to take you out to dinner and we're going to share a fine bottle of wine."

"Why?" she asked.

"Because Faldo didn't pick Darren Clarke."

Nick would be skewered for his picks in the British press. I took heat for my picks as well. Most captains do. That is part of our job. I was there to absorb all criticism before it got to our players. When my picks were made public, Johnny Miller went on a media conference call and said, "You know, I wouldn't have picked any of those guys."

What he didn't know, and wouldn't know until now, is that I didn't pick them either. Their teammates did. And because of that—because I had faith in those guys and empowered them to round out their own pods—I knew we were going into the matches with something America really needed: a cohesive, bonded, sell-out-for-each-other-at-every-turn team.

7

CONTROLLING
CONTROLLABLES

$\mathcal{A}$ lot is made in sports of home-field advantage, and for good reason; the home team has a leg up on its opponents in many ways. The crowd is on your side, and you're in a familiar setting in your own time zone. You know the people guarding the door to the locker room, you get to eat and sleep in familiar surroundings, and you're probably used to the weather and the conditions of the field. Some fields are more favorable to the home team than others. The Red Sox seem to have a huge advantage at Fenway, in part because their left fielder knows how to play caroms off that Green Monster; and when the cold north wind whips through Lambeau Field, opposing teams might as well spot the Packers a touchdown.

Golf is different, although there are still home-field advantages. Very few Americans win the British Open in their maiden voyage,

The "Azinger Cut" would be a topic of conversation all week. The one-inch-deep swath along many of the fairways benefited good ball strikers like Hunter Mahan. During the preparation and competition, Paul would look for opportunities to maximize the assets of our U.S. team. ~ R.B.

and only one European has won the U.S. Open in the last eighty years, Tony Jacklin in 1970. There are exceptions, of course. A good putter from Ireland can win a PGA Championship (Padraig Harrington) just like a patient wind player from Alabama can win the British Open (Stewart Cink). Despite growing up on the links at Royal Troon, Colin Montgomerie has never won his country's open, and there was a period of time in the eighties and early nineties when the Europeans seemed to take over the Masters.

Golf galleries aren't like football fans. You don't boo in golf, and you certainly don't disrupt a swing with deafening end-zone noise. Week in and week out on the PGA Tour, European players have just as many fans as the average American player.

The Ryder Cup is altogether different. Missed putts are applauded by fans of the opposing team. That trend, as jarring as it is the first time you hear it, started in Europe and has now become a part of the matches. On the other hand, birdies are met with whoops and cheers that are indistinguishable from the noise you hear after a touchdown in the Super Bowl. Although we wouldn't be sleeping in our own beds, home-field advantage is huge in an event like this.

I was going to do everything in my power to get the crowd into the matches and make the galleries our 13th man. Our team deserved nothing less, the fans deserved nothing less, and American golf deserved nothing less.

As part of that strategy, I set out to prep the battlefield to give us the best home-field advantage we could have. Valhalla Golf Club was no stranger to big-time championship golf. It had already hosted the 1996 and 2000 PGA Championships. Jack Nicklaus, who designed the course, had made a few touch-ups, adding length and softening some of the more severe greens, but overall the course was not a surprise to anyone. A lot would depend on conditions. The course could be set up to play easy, fair, tough, or impossible. It could also be set up to favor one style of play over another.

Julius Mason told me that in past Ryder Cup matches, the PGA Greens Committee had a specific goal when setting up the courses. "As a rule, Americans have done better in the PGA Championship than the Europeans have," Julius said. "So we've set the Ryder Cup courses to mirror what we do in the PGA Championship."

Historically the captain did not get involved in course setup. I wanted to take a different approach. I wasn't sure what kind of team I would have, but I wanted the option of tailoring the course setup to play up our strengths. I wanted to control the controllables. Europe had had great success setting up their Ryder Cup venues to suit the relative strengths of their teams while trying to neutralize our strengths. I don't know if it was Sam Torrence or the European PGA Tour who set up The Belfry in 2002, but whoever was in charge did a masterful job of tailoring the course to Europe's advantage. At 290 yards off the tee, the fairways narrowed down to the width of walking paths. On some holes, the fairways ended altogether, and a strip of rough ran across the ground right where guys like Phil Mickelson and Tiger Woods would normally hit their tee shots. This took away our bombers' advantage. Everybody played the second shot from the same location, which worked well for the Europeans. They also moved the tee forward on the short par-four tenth hole, a decision that drew some criticism, but it was a brilliant strategic move. Sam's team later acknowledged that they knew the tee would be forward from the beginning, so they practiced hitting high cuts around the tree that blocked direct access to the green. Some of our guys were unsure how to play the hole, because we had practiced from the back tee. Tiger laid up off the tee with an eight-iron and then hit sand wedge into the green all week, which was a smart way to play the hole. But the Europeans drove the ball into the putting surface because they had practiced the hole that way. Those shots got the crowd revved up, energizing the Europeans.

I hoped to do the same thing with Valhalla. With the help of the club's superintendent, Mark Wilson (not to be confused with Mark Wilson, chairman of the PGA of America Rules Committee and chief referee of the 2008 Ryder Cup), we could set up the golf course to play to our strengths. I wouldn't know what those strengths were until I knew who was on the team, nor was I sure how Mark and his staff would respond to my requests. All I knew was that I needed him as an ally. Most golf fans would never hear of Mark Wilson, but everyone would see the condition and setup of the golf course. I hoped to get him to understand what I was trying to accomplish, and how we needed to prep the battlefield to our advantage. I picked up the phone and called Mark early in my tenure.

I could tell right away that he and I were going to get along. I explained to him how the Europeans had clobbered us and how they had set up the course to play to their strength. "The problem is, I'm not sure what our strengths are yet, because I don't know who is on the team," I said. "I don't know if we have great iron players or bombers or what."

Mark immediately understood. "I'm with you, Zinger," he replied.

My first question was, "Is it going to bother you if the guys are making a ton of birdies?"

"Not at all," he answered.

"Good, because I think I want it to be set up to score, so the guys are making birdies and we can get these stands rocking."

Since I was no expert in turf management, I said, "Is it easier to grow the rough high and thick and cut it back, or keep it cut back and grow it high if and when we need it? I'm asking because I won't know for some time if I have a team of bombers or twelve guys who can hit it dead straight, so I don't know what kind of rough I need or how narrow we'll want the fairways."

"I'll tell you, Zinger," Mark said, "it's better to keep it cut. About three weeks out, if we need more rough, we can quit mowing and fertilize the heck out of it, and it'll get a lot longer and thicker."

"Do you mind doing that?" I asked. He had members he had to answer to for two years, so I didn't want to make his life miserable during that time.

"Not at all, Zinger," he said. "My team and I are here for you. We'll do everything we can to help you."

Over the months Mark and I drove around the course several times. One of the things we did when we were together was look for straight lines on the greens. I wanted to be able to say to our players, "Everything right of the pin will be uphill and straight," that sort of thing.

The Europeans had certainly done it in the past. At Valderrama in 1997, Captain Seve Ballesteros knew every inch of the greens. On Saturday morning of that Ryder Cup, as Phil Mickelson was playing the seventeenth, his caddie, Jim "Bones" McKay, discreetly walked around the green looking for the dot of white paint that signified where the pin would be for the afternoon. When he saw a white spot two paces from the front edge, a place where a putt could hit the lip, then roll off the front of the green and into the water, he and Captain Tom Kite walked off shaking their heads and saying, "That's got to be bird [dung]. They can't be putting it there." But they were! Seve put the pin in a spot that might as well have been in a bunker. His players knew it was coming and had prepared. Our guys did not.

Fast forward to 2008. Once it became apparent that our team consisted of a balanced mix of guys who could bomb it off the tee and some of the best iron players in the world, I felt we needed two tiers of rough. Good iron players can control fliers from the short rough, so Mark worked with his staff to cut the rough just enough so that great iron players could control their spin while mediocre iron players could not. The first cut, which varied in width from a five- to fifteen-foot swath just off the fairway, was only an inch high. Beyond that, the rough was about three inches deep. That first cut became affectionately known as the "Azinger cut," and it was one of the most talked-about features of Valhalla the week of the matches, but it helped us play to our strength.

One of the most important things we needed to know (and information that my assistant captains were great about providing) was how far our bombers flew their tee shots. We needed to set the tees so that a well-struck shot would carry most of the trouble. In the case of guys like Phil Mickelson, Kenny Perry, and J.B. Holmes, Mark widened the Azinger cut at the three-hundred-yard mark, because we knew those guys could fly their tee shots that far. J.B. was fifty yards longer than that, so from three-fifty plus, Mark gave him a wide landing area. That part of the fairway wasn't in play for anyone else, so it didn't matter how wide we made it. As for the par threes, my assistant captains asked their guys what their favorite iron yardages were, and we tried to make sure the par threes played within those yardages.

•

Because of the way the tour schedules were loaded in the latter months of 2008, both the European and PGA Tours had an open week prior to the matches. For days I was concerned that the Europeans would come in, play a bunch of practice rounds, and spend a full week smoking cigars, telling jokes, and bonding with each other while our guys were naturally resting at home. So during the negotiations of the captains' agreement, which details rules of the competition, I suggested that Europe would have the course to themselves the Monday and Tuesday in the week prior to the matches, but they would be gone by Wednesday.

Nick agreed. Then I said to Mark, "Hey, Mark, wouldn't it be something if it was so hot that you couldn't mow the greens the Monday and Tuesday that Europe is here playing their practice rounds?"

Mark could read between the lines. The greens rolled about a six on the stimpmeter on those days. As it turned out, it wouldn't matter.

What shocked me was that no European showed up to play a practice round on those early days. Faldo didn't gather his team and have them there, nor did anyone show up on their own, which made me wonder, for the first time, if we were going to face the kind of cohesive European squad we had seen in the past.

We were still making adjustments days before the matches began. Once our guys showed up and started practicing, Mark stood ready to do whatever it took to prep the field for us. During one practice round, I got a call on the radio from Olin Browne who said, "Zinger, you're not going to believe this."

"What is it?" I asked.

"There's a limb out here on sixteen about thirty feet up in a tree that's three hundred yards off the tee. J.B. thinks it might be in his line."

I laughed and said, "Are you kidding? You and I would never see that limb, and he thinks it's in his way?"

"He thinks it is, and the way he's hitting it, he's probably right," Olin said.

So about fifteen minutes later, I got on the phone and called Mark Wilson. "Mark, it's Zinger."

"Hey, what's up, Zinger?"

"Well, there's a limb three hundred yards off the tee thirty feet up that J.B. thinks might be in his way."

"Zinger, Olin's already called me about it," he replied. "I've got a man up in that tree taking care of that limb right now."

"You are the best," I declared. "You've done everything I've asked, and you've been great."

"Thanks, Zinger," Mark said. And as I was about to hang up, he added with a slight chuckle, "Hey, Zinger, that J.B., he's spoiled, ain't he? He's spoiled."

"He is this week," I answered.

As captain, Paul could not predict how our team or how the Europeans would play. However, he wanted to do everything possible to get a home-field advantage within the parameters of the captains' agreement. The course at Valhalla was tuned to the U.S. team's strengths, and they were prepared to know what to expect. When surprises are minimized and players' strengths are maximized, the opportunity for success increases. Here Boo Weekley, with his caddie, Joe Pyland, gets ready to tee off at the second hole, where the tee was set eighty yards forward of its position during the practice rounds. ~ R.B.

•

One of the setup strategies that worked for us was tee placement. In accordance with the captains' agreement, all tees during the matches would be placed at or forward of the stakes that were positioned on each tee. I didn't tell the Europeans exactly where the tees would be, because my hope was that in alternate shot they would have their long hitters teeing off on the even holes. What they didn't know was that I planned on moving the tees up on the even holes and back on the odd ones. On the second hole, for example, one of the longest on the course from the posts, we planned on setting the tee eighty yards forward. We also knew how far our longest hitters flew their tee shots, so I planned on having the tee markers placed so that a well-struck drive would fly over some bunkers. In some cases, we could give a guy like J.B. Holmes a ten-yard buffer, because he flew it so much farther than everybody else.

•

Too often in any endeavor, whether it's business or sports, family or social settings, a small group of people seems to get the accolades. Sure, those people deserve a healthy heaping of praise, but there are always people behind the scenes who don't get the credit they deserve.

As we prepared for the Ryder Cup, Ron and I took a golf-cart ride to the maintenance building where Mark and his staff were working. They had labored for months making sure their course played fair but offered a home-field advantage to the U.S. team. Mark gathered them around outside, and I said, "I know I've asked you all to do a lot. I've asked you to put your egos in check and help set up this golf course in a way that it probably has never been set up before. And you've been willing to do it; you've been willing to do everything I've asked. I want you to know that I appreciate your team. Your team has come together to help *our* team. We've been handed our butts in five of the last six Ryder Cups, and it's difficult to know what the advantage is going to be, but I know I want our guys to be comfortable and not feel handcuffed. You've given them that. You've done everything we've asked, and you've done a phenomenal job. Every one of you has given us the best opportunity we've ever had at home to win these matches. Now it's up to us to do it."

8

MESSAGING

*I*n preparation for the Ryder Cup, Ron and I discussed the importance of communicating with the players according to their behavioral style. What you say to someone and what they hear are often two different things. Not only is tone and expression just as important as what you say but also the timing of your message can influence your relationship with the listener for a long time to come. You might say something quick and short because you're tired or hungry or you have to go to the bathroom, but in the listener's mind you are curt. And that can become the starting point for all future interaction with that person. We've all done this and it often comes back to bite us. On the other hand, a well-placed comment spoken at the right time can make a difference and lead to positive outcomes. A pat on the back or just catching someone's eye and giving him a

On the course Paul crafted his communication to the situation and the player, drawing on his understanding of their unique behavioral styles. Paul also drew heavily upon the experience of veteran Ryder Cup players like Stewart Cink. ~ R.B.

slight nod can reestablish confidence and change an outcome.

As an athlete in the spotlight, I had to be aware of first impressions. Each week I made hundreds of them. If I was running from the range to the locker room to grab a bite to eat, I tried to be aware of the kid looking for an autograph, because even if I didn't see him but he thought I had ignored him, that kid's impression of me would forever be predicated on that one interaction. And if a local cub reporter had a question for me, I tried to give him a complete answer no matter how I felt. He had a job to do, and a few seconds of my time might make that job a lot easier. I like to think answering that question might put me in the "good guy" pile in that reporter's mind.

Many times the difference between what someone says and what the recipient hears can be traced to the personalities of the speaker and listener. An aggressive person might say something he thinks is innocent, but if the listener has a cautious and caring personality, he might hear something totally different. A friend of mine tells a story about his daughter losing a ring in a sink. "She comes in at midnight crying," he said. "Of course she wakes me up. All I could figure out was that she'd been at a ball game, took off her ring to wash her hands, laid it on the edge of the sink, and it fell down the drain. So I said, 'That was dumb, Liz, why didn't you put it in your pocket?' I might as well have confessed to killing puppies. Liz cried. My wife yelled at me. For the next week I was the bad guy. Turns out I had to buy her a new ring just to get out of the doghouse, and I'm still not sure how I got in it."

As the father of daughters I laugh at that story every time I hear it. But the lesson is clear: how you deliver a message is just as important as the message itself. Ron emphasized that to me as we were making final preparations for the matches. "You have to consider these personality types as you message the team," he said. "Each of these players processes information differently. The things you say to a dominant person are not the things you can say to a supportive person. Also, the way you speak to an influencing person is often the opposite of what you would say to a person who is more conscientious."

We've all seen examples of what Ron was saying. Some people respond positively to a direct confrontation and a kick in the backside, while others need a quiet word of encouragement. Our work developing the personality profiles gave me a starting point. Four days together in Louisville before the matches began would give me time to get to know the guys a lot better.

Even before we got to Louisville I saw the process work. When Stewart Cink and Ben Curtis let me know they wanted Chad Campbell for the Steady Eddies pod, my only hesitation was the fact that Chad's wife had just had a baby boy. I knew how difficult those early stages of fatherhood could be. I didn't want to pull him away from his new family if he felt at all conflicted, and I didn't want to put him in a position of feeling guilty about leaving his wife and newborn. So when I called Chad, we small-talked for a minute or two. I congratulated him on his new baby and his good play, then I said, "I need you to be honest with me. If I ask you to be a part of this Ryder Cup team, is having this baby going to affect your preparation?"

He said, "Oh, no sir. I promise you, it won't."

"If I asked you, would you want to be a part of this team?"

He said, "I sure would, Zinger. I wanted to call you and tell you how well I'm driving it, and that I may be hitting it the best I've ever hit it in my life. I promise you'll be happy if you pick me."

"That's all I needed to hear, Chad," I replied. "I am picking you. Now, let me tell you what we're doing." And I filled him in on our strategy.

When I hung up, I turned to Toni and said, "Ron was right."

"Right about what?" she asked.

"Right about how I have to communicate with these guys differently. Chad just admitted to me that he wanted to call and tell me how well he was hitting it, but he wouldn't. If it had been Anthony Kim on the bubble, he would have been calling me twenty times a day."

●

I arrived at Valhalla on Saturday, before the players came in (except for J.B. Holmes, who had come on Thursday). I couldn't help questioning whether I had done everything I could to give my guys their best opportunity for success. On Sunday evening Jim Furyk came through for me with just the right words. Jim had said all along that he wanted to be in a pod with some big hitters, so I had put him with Kenny Perry, Boo Weekley, and J.B. Holmes. As Ron and I looked over the pods, we discussed the fact that those three guys can be hard on themselves if they aren't playing up to their expectations. They might need encouragement from their partner, and Jim can be so focused on his game that he might not naturally think of that.

"I wish you'd brought this up sooner," I told Ron.

"Why don't you call him," Ron suggested.

So I called Jim and got right to the point. "Hey, Jimmy, I need to talk to you about something before you get on the plane. You know I've had Ron doing these personality profiles on everybody. He's telling me we're getting some caution lights with you in the redneck pod."

"Hey, Zinger, man," he said, "you're not going to take me out of my pod are you?"

"Well, I'll tell you, I want to make sure everybody fits just right, but I want to talk to you about it first."

"I think I'm good with those guys. Plus, I've been swallowing vowels and getting all my best redneck sayings down for weeks. 'At ol' boy's so bow-legged he couldn't hem a hog in a ditch.'"

I complimented him on his redneckisms. Then I said, "You know those guys. Sometimes they can be kind of hard on themselves if they hit a couple of bad shots. They might need some encouragement."

"I can encourage those guys," he assured me.

"I know you can do it," I said, "but do you *want* to do it?"

"Absolutely, I do."

"Okay, I'm leaving you in there. I'll see you tomorrow."

I hung up the phone and realized Jim could absolutely be an encourager for his guys. He had just encouraged me.

Ron took it a step further when he said, "Now let me tell you what I've seen. We've been working together for two years, and you've consistently shown what my friend Dudley Lynch calls 'breakthrough thinking.'"

"What's that?" I asked.

"These are creative thinkers willing to take chances, break away from tradition, and look for innovative solutions to complex challenges. They get results by bringing others along with them, selling them on ideas, and making sure to create a win-win environment for everyone. They're willing to share control and empower others not only with responsibility but also with authority to make decisions. They leave no stone unturned and focus on details with intense preparation."

Ron continued with the list, but I got the point. Whether or not I was a "breakthrough thinker," Ron had offered a word of encouragement at the time I needed it most.

I felt confident in our plan, and I had supreme confidence in our players. But I also remembered the prayer that astronaut Alan Shepard said before the launch of Friendship 7, and I repeated it silently to myself. "Lord, please don't let me screw this up."

•

Our guys came in separately. Kenny and his wife drove in from their home in Franklin, and the rest of the team flew in at various times between Sunday and Monday. On Monday I went out to the airport to greet Nick and his squad. There were cameras, of course. The Virgin Atlantic charter taxied onto the tarmac, and I was standing on the concrete wearing a white crewneck shirt and blue jacket, feeling like I was cooling my heels as we waited for them to come down the stairs. When the door to the plane opened, Nick stood in the doorway holding up the Ryder Cup as if triumphant. My competitive juices pushed me to something approaching anger, so much so that Julius Mason, standing beside me, said, "You okay? Smile.

Paul went along with the joke for the camera, but antics like this made him and his players even more determined to bring the Cup home. Without saying a word, Paul's message to the team was sent and received. ~ R.B.

This is the greatest moment of your life." I was also anxious as the European team got off the plane because I realized how strong they were. A few minutes later photographers asked Nick and me to pose for a picture with the Cup, and Nick teasingly held it away from me.

I left the airport more determined than ever to give our guys the best possible chance at success. We had considered every detail, or at least I hoped so. I had let them fill out their pods. I had engaged them in course strategy and setup. I had addressed the little things, asking every player for his three favorite entrées so we could always have something in the team room that they liked to eat. I also had them pick fabrics they thought were most comfortable wearing from a selection Nike had provided, and the company made sure that was the material of their uniform shirts. I hoped my messages, both verbal and nonverbal, were getting through.

•

On Monday afternoon I took the team to the Muhammad Ali Museum in downtown Louisville. The place was awe-inspiring and full of memorabilia. I was growing up when Ali was heavyweight champion and the most famous athlete in the world. He was also someone who always stuck to his beliefs, and for that he is now almost universally loved. I wanted the team to watch the brief film of Ali's life that chronicled his upbringing in Louisville, his ascendancy in boxing, the tough times he had in standing up for his beliefs, and then the comebacks. It was an extraordinary walk through history.

After the film I stood in front of the team and explained, "I wanted you guys to see this, because when I was young, one of the moments in sports that stuck with me for a long time was when Ali fought Ken Norton in 1973. That was the height of his comeback, after being knocked out by Joe Fraser, but before the 'Rumble in the Jungle' with George Foreman. In the second round Norton broke Ali's jaw. Ali never said a word. In fact, he didn't take his mouthpiece out for the rest of the fight because he didn't want anybody to know. The man fought ten more rounds with a broken jaw. Right then I thought, *That's a guy who will never, ever quit.* That memory has stuck with me ever since."

That was all I said, other than, "Okay, let's go to dinner."

I had known for months how critical the next few hours would be. There had been many sleepless nights as I worried about what I would say to this team on this Monday night. Now was the time to make sure they were sold out for each other and for the cause.

After we got back to the hotel, we all gathered in the team room. I asked the wives and the caddies to join us, in part because I wanted all of them to feel like they were part of the team, but also because some of them didn't know about the pod system or the personality profiles we had done. I wanted everyone to hear that message from me, but I didn't want it to get out to the media, and especially to the Europeans. So not only was this session important in terms of making the wives and caddies an integral part of the team but I also hoped to bond everyone with a secret.

The team room was comfortable and relaxed. We always had food in the back. For this meeting, the couches and cushioned chairs were arranged in a right-angled U with a couple of high-top tables and tall chairs behind. Nobody had to stand or strain to see or hear me.

I began at the story's beginning, with me in front of the television, too lazy to turn off the SEAL documentary. I told them how the navy's decision to break the SEALs into small groups within the larger team had led to the vapors of an idea about bringing this team together by breaking it up into pods. Then I said, "Every player in here has had his personality profiled through observation," at which point I introduced Ron to the group for the first time. Some of the players might have recognized him from the galleries, but only Stewart had met Ron. I hoped that by introducing him, giving a synopsis of his background, and letting everybody know his role in the process, the picture would become clear to all.

"I assembled these pods based on numerous phone calls with you guys and personality profiles that Ron has been working on for months," I continued. "We looked at everyone's compatibility based on red light, caution light, and green light scenarios. For example, Phil and Tiger would be a definite red light."

"You didn't have to go there, Zinger," Phil quipped as everybody in the room laughed.

"I also want you to know that Stricker was a consensus pick. Everybody wanted you," I said looking at Steve." The others, Chad, J.B., and Hunter, I want you guys to hear again and the rest of you to know that you were picked by the other members of your pod. They had several options, and they chose you."

The room was quiet, and I let the silence hang in the air. I wanted everyone to hear from me how involved their teammates had been in selecting them. Most of the caddies looked stunned. They were hearing this for the first time. And what I was about to say, I knew they didn't know.

"Guys, this week you are going to be part of a four-man team, or pod. Four of you will bond together this week. Caddies, you are also a part of this pod system. I want you to bond as a unit. I want the eight of you to bond together. You will practice together, play together, and strategize together. You are a team this week. Barring injury or illness, I will never break you apart. Wives, I consider you an integral part of our success. I'm counting on you to tell me the truth about how the guys are feeling, and you can approach me at any time." I also introduced Raymond, Dave, and Olin as my assistant captains and a part of their pods.

Then I got to the part of the message that I would repeat numerous times throughout the week. "I'm not here to tell you how to prepare. You're all big boys, and I'm not going to hold your hand," I said. "I'm your captain, not your coach. Lou Holtz is coming in tomorrow, but we're not going to have a lot of motivational speeches or videos this week. All of you here know there are no shortcuts to success. You can't hope for it. You can't wish for it. It's about preparation. Every one of you is here because you deserve to be here. You are the greatest players in the world. I'm asking you this week to prepare in your small groups. I want you to play great and play aggressive. This is match play not stroke play. You need to be aggressive. I'm asking you this week to embrace this crowd, and let's show off for our people."

I didn't talk about results or winning, even though that was constantly on my mind. I focused on preparation. Then I held up a bag of Ryder Cup lapel pins. "These were my good friend Brandt Packer's idea," I said. Brandt, son of basketball analyst Billy Packer, was my former producer at ABC and is one of the most creative guys I know. He had suggested players hand out lapel pins during the practice rounds.

We had 10,000 lapel pins with the American flag and the Ryder Cup logo on them, and they were something that you could not buy anywhere. In order to have one you had to be at the golf course for the practice rounds. "There are some long walks between holes, and you're going to have people wanting autographs," I said. "Make eye contact with as many people as you can and toss them a lapel pin. It'll keep you moving and allow you to make a connection with this crowd. These fans are our 13th man. Let's embrace them."

I had thought we might have a drum line to get everybody excited about the matches, and that idea had evolved into a Thursday night pep rally. The Ryder Cup had taken on the air of a big-time college football game, so why not have a football-type pep rally with music and cheerleaders? Then we had the added wrinkle of tossing out T-shirts that had "13th Man" printed on them.

Finally I handed out a list of questions and said, "I also want to help eliminate some stress by talking for a few minutes about the media. Here are twelve questions that we are probably going to be asked this week. I've written out how I think we should answer these questions so you don't stress over them. Let's send a consistent message this week and avoid a lot of distractions from the press." I didn't want to control what the players said, but I wanted us to be on the same page when certain questions were asked.

Several of the questions I expected dealt with the fact that Tiger wasn't there. The answers I had written out said, essentially, "We miss Tiger and it would be wrong to say we are a better team without him. Certainly we wish he were here, but he's not, and we're focused on our job this week." As for whether or not Tiger should come to Valhalla to provide moral support, I suggested that we say, "That's up to Tiger. We're just focused on trying to get ready for the week and the matches." In the past Americans have gotten off to bad starts. How will you react if you get off to a bad start? The answer was: "Those were different teams and different players, and we don't feel that has any bearing on us this week." There were others: Hunter Mahan had made some comments about the Ryder Cup that weren't worded exactly the way he might have liked, and even though he'd already apologized, I expected we'd be asked

Phil Mickelson and the rest of the U.S. team took every opportunity to embrace the crowd and show appreciation for the American fans as their "13th man." ~ R.B.

about them again. I also figured we'd be asked about being under-dogs, and the U.S.'s recent Ryder Cup history. By suggesting answers to all these questions, I hoped to make our guys more comfortable and send a consistent message to the media.

Our guys seemed to like keeping the secret of the pod system, even when the media noticed the same groups of four playing every practice round together. Most of us were in the locker room watching a video feed from the pressroom when Boo Weekley was asked who he wanted to play with. He came up with the word of the week. "I like playing with Kenny and J.B.," he said. Then, realizing he might be revealing his pod, Boo quickly added, "Yeah, I can play with J.B., or I can play with Justin or Stricker. Shoot, I can combatibate with anybody."

We laughed about "compatibate" for the rest of the week. Within hours, Julius Mason had a plaque made up that read:

com·pat·i·bate *adj* Middle English, from Medieval Latin, *compatibilate*, literally, sympathetic (from late Latin) *compati*; fifteenth century; Early Spanish explorers to treasure coast–**1:** to cross-fertilize freely or unite vegetatively; **2:** compatible of forming a homogenous mixture that neither separates nor alters from chemical interaction; **3:** capable of being used or connected to other "patibates" that cohabitate the outreaches of the panhandle of Florida; **4:** having a similar disposition and taste, "a compatibate choice of food" with their many similar tastes; "he found her a most sympathetic compatibate"; **5:** able to be jellin' like a felon.

Boo wasn't as backward as he let on. In fact, he was right: we had compatibated.

•

The Louisville crowds were unbelievable. Thousands of people filled the grandstands. They waved flags, cheered, and chanted, "USA! USA!" That was pretty common for the Ryder Cup. Except for one thing: this was during the practice rounds! Never before had I seen a more enthusiastic crowd at a golf event. These people were starving for a win. I saw one sign that said, "The Streak Ends Here. Go USA," and another that said, "PeeEww E.U." The best one was a poster that said, "Enjoy the Barbecue, Nick. The Plane's Going to Be 3 lbs. Lighter on the Way Home Anyway." The Ryder Cup was closer to four pounds, but no need to quibble over such a minor detail. These people were fired up and ready. That was exactly what I had hoped, and exactly what we needed.

On Thursday afternoon chills ran down my arms as we marched in for the opening ceremonies. This was when the emphasis turned onto the players, and they really started to get the recognition they deserved. Every week on the tour these guys were cheered, but never like this. Those cheers started as we walked past the grandstands and continued as we took our seats on the giant stage. This was as close as golfers ever got to being rock stars. But there was more to this than golf. This was about national pride, something very few athletes get the chance to experience.

Nick spoke first. He talked about his parents and his children and how thrilling it was for him to be there. Then he introduced his team, making note of each player's nationality. I was a little stunned when he tried to make a joke by asking Graeme McDowell if he was from Ireland or Northern Ireland. As my daughters might say, you just don't go there.

I kept my remarks brief. I introduced the team, told them how proud I was to be their captain, and thanked the fans of Louisville, telling them how much we looked forward to their support.

Afterward time got a little tight. I felt as though we were losing control of the clock. The schedule called for photos back in the team room after the opening ceremonies, but I didn't realize how long those shots would take. I really got antsy when we all put on football helmets and school jerseys. One of the great things the PGA does is donate $100,000 in each player's name to the college of his choice, but twelve hours before the first match was to tee off, I felt like we needed to wrap up things quickly. I finally said to Julius Mason,

The only time during the week Team USA overrode Captain Azinger occurred when the players and wives decided to attend the Thursday night pep rally in downtown Louisville. This was another example of team unity and the commitment to go all in for Paul and Toni by joining them in embracing the fans as our "13th man." ~ R.B.

"We've got to go. It's getting late, and we've still got the pep rally."

We were hours away from the first tee time, and most players liked to get up at least three hours before teeing off. So I said, "Guys, I've changed my mind. I don't want you going to the pep rally. I'm going to head down there. Get a good night's sleep and let's get ready to play tomorrow."

I rushed down to my room and changed into jeans and one of the 13th Man T-shirts for the pep rally. As I ran out of my room, I went through what I was going to say to the crowd and how I was going to explain the team not being there. When I rode the elevator back up to the team room to get Toni, I was stunned when the doors opened and all the guys and their wives were standing there wearing their 13th Man T-shirts, with Anthony Kim leading the way.

"It's good to see you're following my authority as captain," I said, smiling.

AK said, "We're ready to go, Cap'n."

He couldn't have been more right. They were, indeed, ready to go.

A sea of people crowded into downtown for the pep rally. The University of Louisville cheerleaders were there, as well as Louisville basketball coach Rick Pitino, and Mayor Jerry Abramson. The crowd was estimated at upwards of 15,000, and they were all waiting for us. It looked like an elaborate version of ESPN's College GameDay. The city couldn't have done a better job.

•

We beat the sun to Valhalla on Friday morning, and it wasn't long before the stands were full, which made the pep rally the night before seem all the more poignant. The scene was more like a national championship game than a golf tournament. A surreal moment. In the stands behind the driving range as our guys were warming up, fans were singing "God Bless America." A clean dew still hung on the freshly mown grass, which in a normal golf event would be a serene setting. But long before the first shot was struck, the crowds were as rambunctious as any I'd ever seen. The European fans congregated in the grandstands to the left of the first tee. Thousands were singing, "How'r you going to win without your Tiger?" to the tune of "What are you going to do with the drunken sailor?" The U.S. fans, while greater in number, were not as creative. They boisterously chanted,

"Soccer Sucks! Soccer Sucks!"

Standing on the putting green, Kenny Perry broke the tension by saying, "I guess that's what all those nights in the pub'll get you. They can sing 'em some songs."

AK and Phil Mickelson went out first against Padraig Harrington and Robert Karlsson in foursomes (alternate shot). Harrington got things underway with the opening tee shot that split the fairway. Then Mickelson hit his tee shot in play, and the crowd went wild. My heart was racing as they walked off the tee. These guys deserved every cheer. Several hours later in the morning the noise would grow to a deafening roar when Phil and AK stormed back from a three-down deficit to halve the match and earn a half point.

Our second group, Justin Leonard and Hunter Mahan, also received thunderous applause. The fans really embraced our team. Justin and Hunter were two up through fourteen when Casey, one of Faldo's captain's picks, hit a tee shot in the water on fifteen. A hole later, when Justin rolled in a two-footer, we had a full point on the board.

Right behind Justin and Hunter were Chad Campbell and Stewart Cink, playing against Justin Rose and Ian Poulter. Rose had hit it stiff for a birdie on the second hole and again on the fifth to put our guys two down. I caught them in the rough at the seventh, a par five with two fairways—one to the right that made the hole play longer, and one to the left that was narrower, but which gave the player the opportunity to reach the green in two. Chad had hit his tee shot in the left rough of the lower fairway, so to get to them, Ron and I had to drive across the upper fairway, through the rough, and across a small wooden bridge.

Chad had left Stewart with a terrible lie. When I arrived Stewart was looking to pitch out. He hit a sand wedge that didn't get to the fairway. Chad tried to hit a fairway wood out of the rough and it went in the water. Then Stewart dropped and hit another ball in the water. In the meantime Rose and Poulter waited in the landing area to the right of the green in two. Chad and Stewart conceded the hole without ever reaching the green, and went three down. I got out of the cart and stood on the wooden bridge as they walked toward me, a picture of dejection. What could I say to make a difference and get them refocused before they reached the eighth tee?

I knew I couldn't say the same thing to them that I had said to Anthony Kim, which was, "You're not showing me squat." I needed to say something to them that would play on their steady demeanor. So as they walked up, I said, "Hey, I've got good news and bad news: the bad news is, you've made a ten on this hole. The good news is, you've only lost one hole. You're three down after seven. The way I look at it, Poulter and Rose have everything to lose and you have everything to gain. You remember what Lou Holtz said? W.I.N. stands for What's Important Now. You have a three-hundred-yard walk to decide what that is. I think it's the next shot. Go get 'em."

If I'd said something like that to Anthony Kim, he would have smirked and said, "That's a good one, Cap'n." Yet for Chad and Stewart, I felt it was what they needed to hear. They were the type of people who would understand what Coach Holtz meant. As they walked to the eighth tee, I saw Stewart put his arm around Chad. Later Stewart told Ron that he'd said, "Buddy, let's walk slowly, take some deep breaths, and get ready to play that next shot."

Jim Furyk, right, fist bumps Kenny Perry. Typically, Jim's on-the-course demeanor remains quietly focused and in control at all times. During the week of the Ryder Cup, Jim assumed a leadership role within his pod and was more outgoing, providing verbal support and encouragement to Kenny, J.B., and Boo. ~ R.B.

In the following nine holes, those guys clawed their way to all-square. Then, on the par-five eighteenth, a reachable dogleg right around water with a deep bunker guarding the front of the green, Stewart crushed his drive. Chad looked straight at the flag from 186 yards and was as comfortable as I had ever seen him. He hit a laser five-iron that stopped ten feet from the hole. It was a clutch shot in the kind of pressure situation that few people can imagine.

I jumped up with my arms in the air when Chad's ball hit the green. Then I sprinted out to the fairway, put my arm around Chad, and said, "Buddy, you just gave your little boy a highlight he'll be able to watch for the rest of his life."

His back straightened and I saw a glisten in his eyes. It was the highest praise I could give him, a message Chad would carry with him for the rest of the week and beyond. He deserved it.

The final group of the morning was the most popular. Kenny Perry couldn't take a step without hearing somebody yell, "Go Hilltoppers," the mascot of Western Kentucky University where Kenny went to school. He went out with Jim Furyk against Sergio Garcia and Lee Westwood. It was during that match that I realized how fully Jim had embraced his role as a supporter. When I caught them on the fifth hole, I saw Jim put his arm around Kenny and pat him on the back. He took the message that we gave him and made it his own. Jim had become one of Boo's "inspirators," a job he would relish for the remainder of the week.

Jim would explain his role as "encourager" later. "I usually think about my own game in these team matches," he said, "but in Louisville I was thinking about Kenny, asking his caddie, Freddie Sanders, how Kenny was feeling, whether he wanted me to talk or keep quiet. That's usually not my style, but I tried to put myself in Kenny's shoes, playing before his people in his home state of Kentucky. I had to step out of character a little bit, chatting it up with him. All part of a very interesting week."

Garcia and Westwood scratched out a halve for the Europeans in that last morning match. Still, Kenny and Jim won a half point and we led 3–1 at the lunch break. We had won or halved every match.

In the afternoon fourballs, Phil and AK went out first again and beat Padraig Harrington and Graeme McDowell two up. We lost the second match when Justin Rose and Ian Poulter went crazy and made every putt to beat Steve Stricker and Ben Curtis. But Hunter Mahan and Justin Leonard continued to get hotter. They trounced Garcia and Jimenez 4 and 3.

Finally we put out the other Kentucky boy, J.B. Holmes (who also got a lot of "UK" and "Go Wildcats" chants on every hole), along with Boo Weekley, who had been adopted by everybody. They played Westwood and Søren Hansen. It was the first shots either of them had ever hit in a Ryder Cup, and they both seemed understandably nervous. Earlier in the week when J.B. and I were hanging out in my room at the hotel watching football and talking about all sorts of things, out of the blue he'd said, "I hope somebody ticks me off this week, Zinger."

"Why is that?" I asked.

"'Cause I always play better when somebody ticks me off."

An hour or so into their round, I had just run into our grill room in the Valhalla clubhouse to grab a quick bite. The PGA Tour commissioner was in there along with a couple of PGA of America officials. Everybody was watching the large flat-screen TV mounted on the wall behind the tables. Westwood and Hansen were two up, and my ears perked up when I heard NBC announcer Dan Hicks say that Westwood had been cutting his eyes at Holmes and Weekley as if they were doing something that bothered him. A minute later, I watched J.B. hit his tee shot into the hazard at the par-five seventh.

That's when I got a radio call from Olin Browne out on the course.

"Hey, Zinger, J.B.'s in trouble," Olin said.

"What's wrong?" I asked.

"He's hitting big cuts and big pulls."

As captain, I was in the unique position of being able to give advice to all our players, something that is against the rules in standard stroke-play events. Our assistant captains could not talk to the players during their matches. So I called J.B.'s teacher, Matt Killen, and said, "Hey, Matt, it's Zinger, are you watching?"

"Yeah, Zinger, I'm watching."

"I just got a call from Olin. He says J.B.'s hitting big cuts and pulls. Have you guys worked on that?"

"Yes," he replied. "He needs to come down more from the inside."

"Have you told him that before?"

"Oh yeah, a lot of times."

"Thanks, Matt," I said. "I appreciate you answering the phone."

"No problem."

A minute later, I jumped into my red golf cart, which was parked under the porte cochere, and Ron and I rode down the parking lot, across the street, through the rough, and out to the ninth fairway where J.B. was speed-walking through the rough with his head down. I locked the brakes on the cart, spinning the wheel to the right so I wouldn't throw Ron out. I jumped out straight into my stride before the cart stopped sliding.

"Hey, buddy, slow down a second. I need to talk to you," I called to J.B.

"Yeah, Captain?" he said.

"Hey, you hitting those cuts and pulls today, huh?"

He nodded.

"So, I just called Matty Matt [my nickname for J.B.'s coach] and he says that you need to bring it down more from the inside. Has he ever told you that before?"

"Yeah, he has," he answered.

"Does that make sense to you right now?"

"Yeah, it does."

"Great. Now, slow down a little, take your time, and go show off for your people."

I walked a few more steps with him to make sure he heard what I said next. "Oh, hey," I said, "one other thing: Dan Hicks just said on NBC that Lee Westwood is giving you guys dirty looks. Have you seen that?"

J.B. stopped and I saw fire in his eyes. "He is?"

"I don't know," I said with a shrug. "That's just what they're saying on NBC."

The muscles in J.B.'s jaw started twitching—the desired effect.

"Go get 'em, buddy," I said.

"Bet on it," he declared.

J.B. hit his approach to the ninth hole to within five feet and holed the putt for birdie. On the 605-yard tenth hole, J.B. came out of his shoes on his tee shot. He flew it 362 yards in the air and hit a six-iron over the green. For the rest of the afternoon Westwood and Hansen threw everything they had at our guys, and J.B. and Boo still won half a point.

At the end of day one, we led 5½ to 2½. I hadn't overplayed the importance of a first-day lead, but it felt good to have one for the first time since 1995. Our guys had played great, making birdies everywhere. The crowd was fired up and ready for Saturday. We weren't at the halfway mark yet, but leading by three points after the first day was a lot better than trailing. More important, our guys proved that American golfers could, indeed, bond as a team.

As captain, Paul looked for every opportunity to motivate each player at the right time with the right message. When Paul told J.B. that he was getting dirty looks, you could see the fire rise in J.B.'s eyes. ~ R.B.

These guys had faced some of the greatest pressure in golf and they had risen to the challenge. I couldn't have been happier. As we rode back to the hotel on Friday night there was no doubt that we were a cohesive, enthusiastic, and confident team.

9

RELEASING CONTROL

*I*n interviews prior to the opening matches, I had said I felt like an archer who had been drawing the string of his bow for two years. Now I was letting the arrow fly. After the first day's results, I believed I had it pointed in the right direction.

I've historically been more of an aimer. I guess that was the golfer in me. If you aim at nothing in our game, you're always going to hit it. Reaction is important, but preparation is the key. Aim is a critical part of that. Ron reinforced the message that successful managers, entrepreneurs, and leaders understand that after you create the proper environment and preach the message, you eventually have to trust your aim and let go.

I certainly had to fight the urge to overmanage. At Valderrama, Seve became such a control freak that he almost incited a mutiny.

J.B. Holmes hits out of the rough at six. Saturday matches would test the team's resolve and tempt Paul to change from a captain to a coach. ~ R.B.

By Saturday afternoon of those matches, Colin Montgomerie was saying things like, "He should stay on his buggy and let us play," and when Seve ran maniacally onto the fifteenth fairway, Jesper Parnevik met him halfway and said, "Get away from me!" (That's the edited version.)

There were times when I felt I needed to encourage and support our guys—like telling Chad and Stewart to remember Coach Holtz's W.I.N. message, and firing J.B. Holmes up by letting him know that Lee Westwood was shooting him dirty looks on television. Other times I fought the impulse to step in and say too much. I stayed in the background—often behind the ropes and sometimes completely away from the action. My role was rarely on the fairway or the green. I was a captain, not a coach. A leader, not a teacher.

Structuring the pod system so that we had one assistant captain with each pod—men who were as much a part of that pod as the players—turned out to be an invaluable decision. Having assistants that I trusted implicitly kept me from getting too involved.

The team had done exactly what we'd hoped they would do. They had bonded in their pods. Every player was completely sold out for the other three guys in his group. They were relaxed but focused, prepared but not paralyzed, intense but not overwhelmed. They had embraced the crowd and fed off their energy, pumping fists and making eye contact, just as we had discussed. For some it was easy. Boo, for example, interacted comfortably with the gallery. Every fan was a friend and every roar was like fuel in his engine. He turned and waved his arms to the crowd after every putt fell, and they responded. People related to Boo. He was the fellow in his yard in a T-shirt and flip-flops being interviewed after the tornado; the guy in the hunting section of Walmart teaching a little boy the difference between birdshot and buckshot; the man who, literally, got detained at the airport on his way to the British Open because he'd forgotten to unpack a couple of bullets from his bag. He was everyman. And every man and woman in Louisville loved him.

It wasn't as easy for some of the others. Kenny Perry had to work at engaging the galleries. "I usually get zoned in and try not to let the gallery distract me, because if I get distracted I tend to forget what I'm doing," Kenny said afterward. "So this was totally different for me. But I loved it. Every step I had people cheering for me and calling my name. You don't get that at regular tour events, or even at majors. Sometimes I had to tell myself, 'Okay now, you need to get back to golf,' but it was the greatest experience of my career, no doubt."

After the first day's matches closed, we all went back to the team room where we watched Amy Mickelson and Lisa Cink perform a karaoke rendition of Michael Jackson's "Beat It." The dancing was fantastic. The singing wasn't great, but it was loud. Everybody loved it. The room was tension free. The team was positive.

•

Stewart Cink and Chad Campbell went out first in alternate shot on Saturday, and they promptly ran into a buzz saw. Europe quickly showed why they were heavily favored. Ian Poulter and Justin Rose played light's out. They were five up after seven holes and never gave Stewart and Chad a chance. Our guys played really well and rallied to two down, but they never got closer, losing 4 and 3 to put an early point up for Europe.

Toni Azinger, right, walks down the second fairway with Sarah Holmes and Karyn Weekley following J.B. and Boo. The players' wives were an integral part of the Ryder Cup team throughout the week. On the course they stood by for every shot every day. ~R.B.

In the second match, Justin Leonard and Hunter Mahan fell two down early to Graeme McDowell and Miguel Angel Jimenez. Justin and Hunter had a Muhammad Ali never-say-die attitude and squared the match at fourteen. Then on seventeen, Justin, who was putting like a man possessed, rolled in a fifteen-foot putt that broke a good eight feet. His fist went in the air and he yelled, "That's what I'm talkin' about!" to Hunter. McDowell made a gutsy birdie at eighteen to square the match and earn a half point, but Justin and Hunter got the crowds rolling, which was a boost to everyone else on the course.

Right behind them, we kept AK and Mickelson together for the third straight match. Through six holes they were four up on

On Friday the pairing of Justin Leonard and Hunter Mahan was so dominant, they closed out both of their matches before reaching seventeen. So at the end of the day, Justin and his wife, Amanda, enjoyed a moment walking together up the seventeenth fairway. ~ R.B.

Henrik Stenson and Oliver Wilson, but Wilson, who had never won on the European Tour and was the only player on Nick's squad to sit out all day on Friday, went on a putting tear. This was a clear example of Europe's depth. Wilson was a player most American fans had never heard of, but he single-handedly threatened to take the crowd out of this match. When he rolled in a breaking thirty-footer on the seventeenth, the Euros had unimaginably come roaring back to win their second full point of the morning.

At this point I was struggling. I wanted to jump out of the cart and say something to somebody. I felt I needed to do something to get the guys back on the right track, but I fought the impulse.

Phil Mickelson stands in the woods surveying how to navigate a challenging shot through the trees. There comes a time when a leader must release his grip and trust the plan and players he has put into place. For most of the competition, Paul chose to remain quiet and let the players work in and out of difficulty during their matches. ~ R.B.

Instead I spent a couple of minutes with Raymond Floyd, who had watched every shot. "There's not a lot we can do," Raymond told me. "The guy's birdying every hole. It's one of those things. We didn't make bogeys; they made birdies." Raymond's straightforward, concise assessment calmed me at that point.

Our final group that morning was Kenny Perry and Jim Furyk against Padraig Harrington and Robert Karlsson, a matchup that should have been nip and tuck throughout. But Kenny was as inspired as I've ever seen him. He rolled in putts from everywhere, and our guys took a four-up lead through five holes. Padraig never quit fighting and they cut into the lead. Then Kenny almost made a one on the par-three fourteenth. The roar was so loud you could have heard it in Lexington. He and Jim won the last match of the morning 3 and 1.

After the match Jim walked off the seventeenth green with his arm on Kenny's shoulder, patting him on the back. We couldn't have scripted it any better.

The Euros had nibbled away at our lead on Saturday morning, but we were still ahead 7–5 at the lunch break. I could imagine a lot of fans at home saying and thinking things like, "Oh, no, here they come," but our team never panicked.

J.B. and Boo went out first in the afternoon against Westwood and Hansen, the same matchup that had halved the match the day before. It was a very close match that rocked back and forth, and our guys were one up through thirteen. When Boo rolled in a twenty-footer for birdie at fourteen to go two up, he turned to the crowd with his arms in the air. They responded with another incredible eruption. By Saturday afternoon, the chant for his group had morphed into "Boo-S-A. Boo-S-A." Our fans might not have pub songs, but they could be creative on the fly.

Boo and J.B. won 2 and 1, handing Lee Westwood his first Ryder Cup defeat in thirteen matches, a streak that equaled a record held by Arnold Palmer.

A three-point lead with three matches left on Saturday gave us a little breathing room. Our team and the Euros were clicking on all cylinders, and birdies flew all over the course in the middle two matches. Steve Stricker and Ben Curtis went punch for punch with Sergio Garcia and Paul Casey. Every time Sergio would hole a putt and display the histrionics that have made him famous, Stricker would pour one in right behind him.

Behind them Kenny and Jim were back out against Poulter and McDowell. Kenny almost aced the fourteenth for the second time in the same day, and his birdie won the hole. Now just one back, Jim hit his approach to an inch on the fifteenth, but McDowell responded with a five-foot birdie putt to halve the hole and maintain the lead. Our guys were nine under, but the Euros were still one up with three to play in that match.

Our final group of the afternoon was Mickelson and Hunter Mahan against Stenson and Karlsson. It was Phil's fourth match, which meant he would play every session. That's a grueling regimen, especially under the intense glare of the Ryder Cup. But I had already asked Amy Mickelson if she thought Phil could go all five matches. I didn't ask Phil, because I knew he would insist that he was ready. The wives always knew, and they would tell you the truth. I'd been diligent in involving the wives. As far as I was concerned they were as much a part of the team as the players and caddies. Amy assured me that Phil was not only ready but anxious to go, so I changed up his pairing and put him with Hunter. AK's hip was giving him a little trouble, and Hunter had been playing great, so I felt good about this match in every respect.

It turned out to be a barn burner. Karlsson birdied five out of seven holes to keep things all-square through fourteen.

With the three final groups playing the final four holes, they all could have gone either way. In blackjack the casino has a 1-percent edge over the player. In championship golf, it can be even closer. Our goal from the beginning had been to create an environment that pushed the razor-thin edge in our direction. We were all-square in two matches, and Kenny and Jim were one down. If we lost all of them, the Europeans could tie things up at eight points apiece and gain a lot of positive momentum going into the singles matches. It was a crucial time, and the fans knew it.

Stricker and Curtis were the first group to reach the par-five eighteenth, and they were all-square. It had been as tight and well played a match as we had seen all week, but it was critical that we get away with some points. Boo and J.B.'s match was over, but the other matches were lined up directly behind Stricker and Curtis. It looked like all of them would come down to the final green. Momentum, and perhaps the outcome for the week, could be determined right here.

Ben hit his tee shot far left and was unable to recover. That left everything up to Stricker. I was standing short and left of the green with Dave Stockton, who seemed completely unruffled by the magnitude of the situation. I was pacing around like a cat. Stricker hit an incredible third shot from the tall fescue right of the green. He left himself an uphill eighteen-footer for birdie. It was a must-make situation. Casey had a ten-footer.

Stricker looked at the putt from every angle, while I watched and tried to breathe normally standing just inside the gallery ropes with Dave. It was amazing how quiet the crowd could be in a tense moment like this. Then Stricker hit one of the most solid putts of his life. The putt broke two feet left to right and into the center of the cup. The crowd behind the final green went berserk. It was the most crucial shot of the matches so far, and everybody in the gallery knew it.

Steve Stricker's up-and-down for birdie at the par-five eighteenth on Saturday afternoon ensured a crucial half point for the team. Steve and Ben Curtis were all-square with Sergio García and Paul Casey as they teed off at eighteen. Steve's chip hit a bank that kicked the ball fifteen feet past the hole. Casey and García were both closer, ten and seven feet from the hole, all putting for birdie. Steve made his birdie putt (opposite page), shifting the pressure to the Europeans. ~ R.B.

Paul Casey made his birdie putt to halve the hole and the match, but we got out with a half point, which meant we were assured of going into Sunday with a lead.

A couple of minutes later, after Stricker and Curtis shook hands with their opponents and waved to the still-frenzied crowds, I ran up and put a hand on Stricker's shoulders. "Buddy," I said, "there is only one other person on the planet who could have made that putt, and he's sitting at home with a busted knee."

Kenny and Jim poured it on, birdying five of the last six holes, but McDowell and Poulter one-putted twelve of the last thirteen greens for eight birdies and four pars. Then Poulter holed the birdie putt on the final green that won a full point for Europe. That left one group on the course, our aggressive guys, Mickelson and Mahan, all-square with Karlsson and Stenson. Hunter's eighteen-foot eagle putt on eighteen missed by an inch. Then Karlsson made his sixth birdie of the back nine to halve the hole and the match.

We got out of the afternoon with a 2–2 split. That meant we would go into the Sunday singles matches leading 9–7.

Remarkably, it was the first time in thirteen years that we had taken a lead into Sunday. I praised our guys for staying true to their mission and coming through when things got tight. Now I had to come up with the proper order for our singles matches.

10

FINISHING STRONG

$\mathcal{H}$istorically Americans had done better in singles, although not recently. We had led this Ryder Cup from the opening bell, but we had been clocked in singles in 2002, 2004, and 2006. Anything could happen.

Five minutes after the last group finished on Saturday, I walked into the clubhouse. In our team area everybody was in some stage of eating, either sitting at a table or standing in the buffet line. They were famished after a long day on the course. It was quiet. I congratulated everybody on their fantastic play. We had less than an hour after the conclusion of Saturday's play to submit our Sunday order. Neither captain knew what the other captain was doing in terms of who would go out when—we both put our lists in an envelope and handed them to officials who would be waiting outside the

The grandstand behind the first tee was already jammed Sunday morning when Anthony Kim teed off against Sergio Garcia. Paul planned for the singles play on Sunday to be in the order of their pods. However, he wanted the team to have ownership of that decision and stay strong till the end. ~ R.B.

door. Out on the course I had already written the order I wanted for the singles matches, and I'd shown it to Ron before meeting with the players. I had a plan, but I also felt like this was not the time to dictate to the team. We had worked so hard at making this an all-in process that I hoped the players would to come to the same conclusion I had regarding the Sunday order.

I sat down at one of the few empty tables. I took out a blank sheet of paper and asked the assistants and players to gather around. When everybody was close, I leaned back in my chair, put my hands behind my head and my elbows out, and said, "We've got about forty-five minutes to get our order in, and we've got some choices. We can put the six veterans out first and anchor with the rookies (this was the first Ryder Cup for six guys) or we can put the six rookies out first and anchor with the veterans. We can go out willy-nilly, or we can go in the order of our pods."

Mickelson, sitting just to my right, swallowed whatever he was eating as quickly as he could and said, "I think we should go out in the order of our pods."

Furyk and Cink quickly agreed, followed by the rest of the team. It was unanimous.

"Great, so do I," I said. "We have a two-point lead; what do you think about putting the aggressive pod out first?"

Phil jumped in and said, "I love it."

AK was the only player not in the room. He was back at the hotel getting a treatment on his hip. We all agreed that he should go out first.

I looked at Phil and asked, "How would you like to anchor your pod and go out fourth?"

"Great."

There was a short debate over whether Hunter or Justin should go out second, so I suggested, "Why don't we have the two rookies go out first and have the two veterans anchor the first pod." That meant Hunter would follow AK, and Justin would go out third in front of Phil.

Heads nodded.

Then I said, "How about we send Kentucky out in the middle?" Again they agreed. I turned to Kenny Perry and asked, "KP, how do you feel about following Phil?"

He answered, "That's great."

To Furyk I said, "Jimmy, what do you think about anchoring your pod?"

"I'd be happy to."

Then I looked at Boo and said, "Boo, I want to sandwich you between Kentucky," and to J.B., "That means you're out number seven."

J.B. and Boo smiled and gave each other a high five.

One pod to go. It was clear in my mind that Cink and Stricker were playing the best within the steady/supportive pod. I looked at Stewart and asked how he felt about leading his pod and following Furyk. He answered, "I would love to be in that spot."

Then I looked at Steve and asked, "Are you comfortable following Stewart?"

"Yes."

I knew at that time I had three of my hottest players in the most vulnerable spots. In most Ryder Cups, the outcome is decided by the eighth, ninth, or tenth singles match. With two confident players remaining, the only question was: Who did I want to burden with the twelfth spot? I looked at Campbell and said, "Chad, I'm thinking about putting you out twelfth. The outcome rarely comes down to the twelfth man. I've been in that position before, against Faldo in 1993. It's a nervous place to be, but I think you can handle it."

"I love it," he replied. "I can handle it. I'll be fine."

I looked at Curtis and said, "That puts you out eleventh, Ben."

He nodded and said, "Okay."

"We all agree?" I asked. It was a unanimous yes.

That was how we did it. I folded the paper as I walked, put it in the envelope, and handed it to the official. Then I walked into the locker room, plopped down in front of my locker, and let out a sigh of relief. As I started to change my shoes, Ron came in and sat down beside me with a big smile on his face. I pulled out the sheet of paper I had written in the cart. It was the exact same order the players had agreed was best.

"That's your leadership style," Ron said. "Some leaders would have slapped down their list and said, 'This is the way it's going to be.' You brought everybody in, asked questions, and made them a part of the process. You ended up where you wanted to go, but how you got there makes a huge difference."

Now it was a matter of seeing Faldo's list and looking at who would play whom. We headed back to our rooms for a quiet night. No motivational speeches were planned; none were needed. We hung out and ate a little more, then signed a few pin flags, hats, and posters for each other and turned in early.

That night, lying in bed, I wondered aloud if I should have said or done something more.

"No," Toni said. "They're ready."

•

The stands were rocking on Sunday morning, not just on the first tee. Fans filled the grandstands out on the back nine as far away as the fourteenth and fifteenth holes by 10 A.M., four hours before a single golfer would walk by them. I had never seen that level of enthusiasm from a golf gallery. The fans had embraced their role as our 13th man. I truly felt like they had become a part of our team.

They certainly gave AK a rousing ovation when he got things rolling. He was playing Sergio Garcia, which fulfilled his wish. He had said all week that he wanted to play Sergio. After splitting the first fairway, AK hit his second shot to two feet. Then Sergio hit his second shot three feet from the hole. As they walked onto the green, Sergio looked at AK and said, "Good, good?"

AK smiled and responded, "No, let's putt them."

He didn't say, "I've seen you putt," out loud, but the message was clear. AK was taking no prisoners. Sergio made his three-footer and gave AK his two-footer to halve the hole in birdies, but the tone of the match had been set.

AK birdied the second by hitting an approach that looked like it was going to fly in the hole. That put him one up. From there he never looked back. He began the day with four consecutive threes, eagled the seventh, shot 30 on the front nine, and was three up at the turn. In addition to flustering Sergio, AK whipped our crowd into a frenzy.

In the second match out, Hunter Mahan drew Paul Casey. They both played great, and the match went back and forth from a two-up to a one-up lead for Hunter throughout most of the round. At that point, the size of the lead really didn't matter. The scoreboards, which were everywhere, showed two groups out and two red-white-and-blue flags on the board. It was the kind of early momentum that could be contagious.

Justin Leonard teed off third against a red-hot Robert Karlsson, who had won the week before the matches and had already made a slew of birdies in this Ryder Cup. It looked like the big Swede decided to have another career round. Karlsson was 3-under on the front nine, and had Justin down early.

Phil also had some trouble in his match against Justin Rose. Five matches in a Ryder Cup are tough, and I couldn't fault Phil for running on fumes by Sunday afternoon. Statistically, players who play all five matches lose in singles more than 75 percent of the time. Thankfully by the time Phil went one down on the sixth, Kenny Perry, who was playing right behind him against Henrik Stenson, had a three-up lead.

I was on the first tee for the start of every match on Sunday, reiterating our message. I said, "Play to play great. Play aggressive and show off for the crowd." When Boo walked up, I came up beside him and asked, "How do you feel, buddy?"

He smiled and cocked his head, "I'm a little nervous, Mr. Zinger."

"You should be, man," I said. "This is a big stage, but look around."

As Boo turned and scanned the crowed, I added, "These are your people. Go show off for your people today."

Boo rides his driver off the first tee. His unbridled spirit and enthusiasm was infectious and greatly contributed to team unity. ~ R.B.

As he walked to the tee, he looked up into the grandstands. I saw him smile as he stood over his opening tee shot. I thought, *Wow, I didn't know Boo smiled over the ball.* Little did I know what he was about to do. He and his wife had talked about what might come next. He would later say, "I'd picked me out a spot, and said that if I hit it, I was gonna ride that driver like a horse off that first tee, Happy Gilmore style."

Boo ripped his tee shot right onto his spot. The crowd went nuts, and Boo straddled his driver and rode it off down the walking path. By this time the grandstands were shaking. I'd always heard thunder analogies when people talked about crowd noise, but I couldn't fully appreciate it until that moment.

He was understandably excited after riding his driver off the tee, and he looked a little quick when I saw him tug his approach shot into the first green. I hustled out and caught him in the fairway and said, "Buddy, that was the funniest thing I've ever seen in my life. Now, I know you're excited, but I need you to settle down and settle in. Can you settle in for me?"

"Yes, sir," he said, nodding.

"Great. Go get 'em."

Boo shot 29 on the front side and was four up through ten holes.

Nick put his strongest veterans, Westwood and Harrington, out last. That strategy backfired. By the time they teed off, we were leading in six matches, the Europeans led in three, and one was all-square.

The crowd rallied and our players responded. Kenny Perry was so nervous that he called Henrik Stenson "Henry" all day. If it had been anybody else, you might have thought it was gamesmanship, but Kenny is the nicest guy in the world and would have cut off his hand before he'd game anybody. Still, after Kenny birdied the third hole to take a two-up lead, Stenson looked at him with those Arnold Schwarzenegger "Terminator" glasses and said in a thick accent, "You're not going to make it easy on me, are you?"

Kenny smiled and answered, "I like you and all, Henry, but today's the most important day of my career."

In fact, Kenny not only thought this Ryder Cup would be a perfect capstone to his career, but he also thought it might even define his career. And he played like it. He was three up at the turn and showed no sign of backing off.

Ron and I were riding along on the back side of the course before any players got there. The PGA had done a great job of placing big screens around the course so fans could follow the action on multiple holes. Fans also had earphones and small transistor radios that broadcast the audio of the NBC and BBC coverage, so it was easy for everyone to know what was going on. I pulled the cart into the middle of the thirteenth fairway, jumped out, made an exaggerated wave with my arms toward the scoreboard, which was full of American flags, and then pointed to the fans and gave them a round of applause. After two years, letting go and watching it all come together was one of the greatest moments of my life.

AK put the first point on the board when he closed out Sergio with an eight-foot putt for par on the fourteenth. He was so caught up in the moment that he didn't realize he'd won. He marched off the green and headed toward the fifteenth tee as Sergio and assistant captain José María Olazábal laughed at him. Once he realized what he'd done, AK charged back and gave Sergio a handshake and a hug.

There are twenty-eight total points available in the Ryder Cup. We needed 14½ points to take the Cup away from Europe. AK's win made the overall score 10–7, and we led in five other matches—but the Europeans led in five as well. The razor-thin edge was becoming as thin as ever. Of our leads, only Boo Weekley's match was a blowout. He led four up after ten holes, and had halved eleven and twelve, getting closer and closer to closing out Oliver Wilson.

The next point went to Europe when Karlsson made his fourth birdie of the day at the fifteenth hole to beat Justin Leonard. That made it 10–8. Only a minute or so later, Paul Casey made a birdie putt at sixteen to square his match with Hunter. I knew Hunter's point was pivotal. Like Stricker's and Curtis's match late on Saturday, Hunter's match could go either way, and it could shift momentum one way or the other.

I needed to be out there to see Hunter come up seventeen, but I was out of position. The crowds were so thick that in order for me to watch, I had to plan ahead. To see Hunter putt on seventeen, I found myself speeding in the cart past the eighteenth green toward the tee, realizing I was going to have to park on the eighteenth tee and navigate another thirty yards through hundreds of people to get to the seventeenth green.

I was listening on my headset and heard that both guys bombed huge tee shots, although Hunter's ball found the light cut of rough. He was first to play, and he hit it to the front of the green, leaving himself a tough forty-foot putt for birdie. Casey hit his second shot pin high eighteen feet away.

I jumped out of the cart and sprinted toward the green as Hunter was about to putt. I was still out of position, twenty rows deep. A couple of guys were surprised to turn around and see me straining to see over them. A few moved aside to let me get closer, but the crowds were just too thick. I leaped in the air in time to see Hunter hit the putt. It looked good leaving.

I heard the crowd noise begin to build. I jumped again just in time to see the ball go in the hole.

That was when sound had feel. The crowd eruption reverberated against my chest like a shock of wind in an air tunnel. Then I jumped once more, this time to catch Hunter's reaction as he pumped both fists in the air and screamed back at the gallery.

Paul arrived at seventeen just in time to see Hunter Mahan make his forty-foot putt. The essence of team building is to successfully lead others to achieve their highest level of performance and reap the rewards of victory. ~ R.B.

I inched my way forward in time to see Casey leave his eighteen-footer well short. Hunter had gone one up with one to play. In his fifth match in three days, he was assured of at least a half point, a critical halve at a time when momentum could have gone either way.

Casey hit a great second shot onto the green at the eighteenth and won the hole with a birdie to halve the match with Hunter. But thanks to Hunter's gutsy play, we were a half point closer to victory with things falling our way late.

At about the same time Hunter was taking off his cap and shaking Paul Casey's hand, Phil was shaking hands with Justin Rose, who had closed things out 3 and 2 to give Europe another point. That added a new level of importance to Kenny Perry's match, which Kenny had controlled from the get-go. Things got tight late though. Stenson made a birdie at the par-three fourteenth to cut Kenny's lead to two up with four holes to play. Kenny got it right back with a birdie at the fifteenth to go dormie with three holes left. Fifteen minutes later, a routine par sealed it. Kenny won 3 and 2, and the applause for Kenny from the Kentucky faithful was unbelievable. He held both arms aloft to thank the fans who had supported him from the beginning.

That's when eighty-two-year-old Ken Perry Sr., wearing a team shirt underneath his cleanest overalls, shuffled out onto the sixteenth green to hug his son. The cheers went up again as father and son embraced. There wasn't a dry eye within a hundred yards.

Minutes later Boo closed out his match against Wilson 4 and 2 with an emphatic birdie at sixteen. "Boo-S-A" reverberated throughout the course.

At that point I was trying to calculate how we stood. It was looking good. I wanted to be there when we secured the Ryder Cup, and I wanted as many of our guys as possible to be there with me.

•

With Kenny's match finished, the Kentucky fans flocked to watch J.B., and they got one of the best shows of the day. All-square with Søren Hansen through fifteen, J.B. pulled his tee shot at sixteen into the rough. It didn't matter though. The guy had bombed it so far past everyone that he only had a wedge left to a hole that was 511 yards long. That's when I noticed J.B.'s breathing. After Friday, J.B. and I had been signing some things in the team room and he admitted, "I had trouble controlling my adrenalin today."

"Adrenalin is the real thing," I told him. "I didn't learn how to win until I learned how to control my heart rate. I did that by learning to control my breathing."

J.B. asked how I did it, and I told him that I inhaled to the count of four, very slowly, and exhaled to the count of four. When I saw him on sixteen on Sunday, J.B. was taking slow breaths—in: one, two, three, four, and out: one, two, three, four. I felt confident that he was in control.

It was shocking how far J.B. could hit the golf ball, and the look of steely determination on his face told all of us that he was not about to let up. With the crowd buzzing in the background, J.B. hit his wedge to six feet.

J.B.'s routine rarely varies. He takes a long time looking at his putts, and he has his caddy stand behind him to make sure he's got all his lines right. But once his caddy moves away, he hits the putt immediately. The six-footer at sixteen was good all the way. When it hit the hole, the crowd went crazy again. J.B. was one up, and it looked like he would be the guy to clinch the Cup.

Hundreds of people ran down the gallery areas beside the seventeenth fairway to watch J.B. and Hansen. It almost looked like the start of the Boston Marathon. I plowed ahead in my golf cart, stopping on a hill beside the seventeenth green. J.B. teed off first. When he hit his tee shot, I heard whoops from the gallery behind the tee. For a second I thought I must have missed the ball, because I hadn't seen it come down. Then I realized that was because it hadn't come down yet.

When the ball finally landed, I fell out of the cart laughing. "Who can hit it that far?" I asked. J.B. had just driven it 400 yards! It was not only the longest tee shot of the week but maybe the longest in Ryder Cup history. He had a half sand wedge second shot from seventy-eight yards on a 478-yard hole.

Hansen was well behind J.B. off the tee. He hit what looked like a great approach, but it flew over the flag and ran off the back of the green, leaving him with an incredibly difficult shot.

J.B.'s approach wasn't easy, even though it was short. He had to finesse a wedge over a large bunker, the kind of touch shot that is especially tough under pressure. And this was pressure. We weren't sure if this match would decide the Ryder Cup, but it was looking like it might.

J.B. took a couple of practice swings, stared down the flag, and hit one of the most deft short approach shots I've ever seen. The ball flew a couple of feet over the bunker and stopped within two feet of the hole.

As J.B. was pumping his fist in air for the fans, it was only appropriate that Johnny Miller called it "the best shot of his career." Hansen made us all catch our breath when his chip for birdie lipped out. Then J.B. made his putt for the match.

Right behind them, Furyk was two up with two to play on Miguel Angel Jimenez. One more half and it was over. I was glad we didn't have to move. Thousands of people lined the seventeenth fairway and crowded behind the green when Jim and Miguel hit their tee shots in the fairway.

Throughout the week, Paul emphasized a focus on preparation versus results. However, once the Ryder Cup was reclaimed, the celebration began. Paul was quick to acknowledge and recognize the players who deserved the credit for the U.S. team victory. ~ R.B.

Miguel played first and hit his approach shot to twenty feet. Jim hit his second shot a little bit farther away, leaving himself twenty-five feet to secure the win. Jim didn't make his putt, but he left it within tap-in range. Miguel needed to make his to extend the match. It took a while for him to putt. The crowd was understandably rambunctious. But when he missed his putt, it was over. Jim's putt was conceded.

Wives, caddies, and players leaped in unison. Toni threw her arms around my neck and I squeezed her tight.

With the mission accomplished, Paul had a tremendous sense of relief from the pressure. The celebration provided a feeling of elation from achieving his goal to reclaim the Cup for the United States and fulfill his purpose as Ryder Cup captain. ~ R.B.

We had done it. The United States had won the Ryder Cup!

With the outcome decided, Ben and Chad both won their matches, giving us a margin of victory of 16½ to 11½, the biggest win for the U.S. since 1981.

•

Celebrating our victory on the balcony of the Valhalla clubhouse will remain a cherished memory for the rest of my life. In three days our guys had played as brothers, leaving everything on the golf course for each other, for me and the assistant captains, and for their country. Now as we stood among the flags and basked in the cheers of fans all around, I couldn't help but reflect on this two-year journey.

The State of Kentucky had treated me like a hero from the day I was named captain, with dinners at the Governor's Mansion, an introduction at center court of the Kentucky-Louisville basketball game, royal treatment at the Kentucky Derby, and a personal visit with Muhammad Ali.

From across the United States we drew encouragement. President George W. Bush invited me to the Oval Office, I threw out the ceremonial first pitch at the American League Championship Series game between the Tampa Bay Rays and the Chicago White Sox, and I was invited to ring the closing bell at the NASDAQ stock exchange.

Everywhere I went during those two years, people, often total strangers, offered encouraging words in the hope that we could achieve this moment together.

The cheers started up again: "U-S-A! U-S-A! U-S-A!" Sometimes in a quiet moment, they still echo in my memory.

Spectators reminded both teams who they were playing for as they waved their American and European flags at the opening ceremony.

When Paul Azinger arrived at the seventh hole on Friday morning, Stewart Cink and Chad Campbell were already two down and in trouble again. Chad's drive had found deep rough. Paul and Stewart discussed the best way to play out of the rough. Paul thought Stewart could hit a sand wedge over the big rock in front of the ball and into the fairway. Stewart was less certain.

Stewart took Paul's advice, trying to go over the rock with his sand wedge. The ball hit the rock and stayed in the rough. "That was one of the most important lessons for me, and I'm glad it came early in the match," Paul said later. "I wasn't there to tell these guys how to play golf. They were already the best in the world. My job was to encourage them, create an atmosphere where they could perform at their highest level, and then stay out of the way."

Stewart and Chad lost the hole but fought back to win their match against Ian Poulter and Justin Rose one up.

After winning three straight holes to square the Friday morning match, Phil Mickelson and Anthony Kim agreed to stay aggressive and keep the pressure on Padraig Harrington and Robert Karlsson. AK's drive on the 511-yard par four sixteenth hole settled in the "Azinger Cut," one-inch rough on the left side of the fairway. Here he and Phil discuss their options. Phil's four-iron from the rough came up short of the green, then Kim nearly holed the chip, forcing Harrington to make a twelve-foot par putt to halve the hole.

At the ninth hole on Friday morning, Kenny Perry followed Jim Furyk's drive with this shot to five feet from the pin.

Jim Furyk, right, and Kenny Perry, celebrate with their caddies, Mike Cowan, left, and Fred Sanders, after Kenny made a sixteen-foot putt for birdie at twelve on Friday morning. Sergio Garcia missed his fifteen-footer, and the Americans went two up on the match.

A charged-up Boo Weekley after chipping in from forty feet on the edge of the green for birdie at the twelfth hole in Friday afternoon.

Much of the joy of the Ryder Cup is cheering your teammates. Boo Weekley stuck his approach shot two feet from the pin on the 511-yard par four sixteenth hole to the cheers of Nicki Stricker, Steve Stricker, Pam Browne, Phil Mickelson, Anthony Kim, Lisa Pruett, Sandy Perry, Lisa Cink, Hunter Mahan, and Stewart Cink.

J.B. Holmes hits from the rough in Friday afternoon fourballs. He and Boo Weekley would halve their match with Lee Westwood and Søren Hansen.

Fellow Spaniards Sergio García, left, and Miguel Ángel Jiménez played together only once during the four Ryder Cup matches on Friday and Saturday, while the U. S. strategy was to maintain the same pairings throughout foursomes and fourballs play.

The long bridge at the sixth hole became a place of contemplation for many of the golfers, especially on Friday and Saturday, when the U.S. and European teams combined for nine bogeys and only one birdie, by Anthony Kim on Friday afternoon.

Padraig Harrington hits out of the fairway bunker at the eighteenth hole during Friday afternoon fourballs.

Justin Leonard's approach at fifteen on Friday afternoon hung up in the rough near the green. From there he chipped in for birdie. Sergio García and Miguel Ángel Jiménez missed birdie attempts, leaving Justin and Hunter Mahan with a 4 and 3 win.

Former President George H. W. Bush and basketball great Michael Jordan were among the spectators cheering for the U.S. team.

When Anthony Kim's tee shot on twelve found the woods, Phil Mickelson's recovery shot rattled around and stayed in the trees. Meanwhile, Henrik Stenson and Oliver Wilson played the hole perfectly, squaring the Saturday morning foursomes match after being down 4-0.

Stewart Cink, center, and Chad Campbell wait on the fourteenth green alongside European captain, Nick Faldo. The Americans bogeyed the hole.

Phil Mickelson made a snaking eighteen-foot eagle putt at seven to give him and Hunter Mahan a 3-1 lead over the Europeans during Saturday afternoon fourballs. Phil had played three match- es paired with Anthony Kim, but AK's hip was giving him problems on Saturday afternoon. Phil and Hunter made a formidable pairing.

Ben Curtis tees off at five in Saturday afternoon fourballs. He and partner Steve Stricker had lost 4 and 2 on Friday, but they matched Sergio García and Paul Casey hole for hole on Saturday afternoon.

Hunter Mahan tees off at twelve on Saturday afternoon. After three matches paired with Justin Leonard, two wins and a halve, Hunter was paired with Phil Mickelson on Saturday afternoon. Phil made four birdies and an eagle, and Hunter made three more birdies to halve their match with Henrik Stenson and Robert Karlsson, who made six birdies in a seven-hole stretch.

Lee Westwood putts at the beautiful thirteenth hole on Saturday afternoon. His partner, Søren Hansen, birdied the hole to pull within one hole, but Boo Weekley followed with a birdie at fourteen. He and J.B. Holmes won 2 and 1.

European and American fans were boisterous and sometimes outlandish.

Jim Furyk's birdie putt at seventeen was one of six birdies he made on Saturday afternoon. And not one of them let him win a hole, as he and Kenny Perry were locked in a classic match with Ian Poulter and Graeme McDowell. The Europeans won the match 1 up, as Jim and Poulter both birdied eighteen.

The American team held a 9–7 lead when play began on Sunday morning. Justin Leonard tees off at the fourth hole against Robert Karlsson. The Americans would win seven of twelve singles matches, with one halve.

Ben Curtis finished off five-time Ryder Cup veteran Lee Westwood 2 and 1 with a birdie at seventeen. Ben had fallen two down after ten holes, then roared back to win five of the next seven holes and take the match.

Sunday was a joyful day for the Americans.

Amy and Phil Mickelson walk up the fairway wrapped in an American flag celebrating the U.S. victory.

Toni and Paul Azinger take a victory lap in the Captain's Cart.

During the celebration on the clubhouse balcony, J.B. Holmes and Dave Stockton hold up the arms of Captain Azinger symbolizing how the players and assistants joined together to support their captain in leading the team to a decisive victory.

For Paul, winning the Ryder Cup was about creating strong relationships. The strongest relationships in his life are his family, and they celebrated his joy on Sunday night. With him are, from left to right, daughter Josie Lynn; wife, Toni; daughter Sarah Jean; and son-in-law, Tim.

The team joined Paul in thanking Mark Wilson and his entire grounds crew for their work preparing the golf course and setting it up to play to the strengths of the United States players.

The winning U.S. team with the Ryder Cup trophy following the closing ceremony, clockwise from top center: Captain Paul Azinger, Stewart Cink, Chad Campbell, Steve Stricker, Justin Leonard, J.B. Holmes, Hunter Mahan, Anthony Kim, Ben Curtis, Boo Weekley, Jim Furyk, Kenny Perry, and Phil Mickelson.

RESOURCES FOR YOU

The players on the U.S. 2008 Ryder Cup team responded to the challenge before them as well as any group of athletes in history. Our job was to implement a strategy that would create the best environment to succeed. The principles we applied specifically to golf offers a template for personal growth and building effective teams. Focusing on relationships produces positive results. Team unity comes by understanding the unique behavioral style and contribution of each person. Giving responsibility and authority fosters trust and confidence. And, finally, messaging people according to their needs and not our own encourages peak performance. These are some keys to success not just for sports, but in business and life.

The principles are clear, but aren't always easy to implement. Paul's message was: "There are no shortcuts to success. You can't wish for it. You can't hope for it. It's all about preparation." And that, we know you can do.

You're probably not leading twelve world-class golfers in an international match watched by 600 million people. Instead, you might be leading a sales team, a management group, or most important your own family. Whatever your situation, the winning strategy we implemented at the Ryder Cup can be adapted to crack the code for your own personal goals.

Make it work for you.

To receive information about speaking engagements, golf outings, personality assessment tools and team-building training, please contact us at:

TCP SPORTS MANAGEMENT
3300 Windy Ridge Parkway · Atlanta, Georgia 30339
e-mail address: www.TCPSports@gmail.com
phone contact: 1-404-961-5154
